First edition published April 2016

Oftwominds.com
P.O. Box 4727
Berkeley, California 94704

Cover: Theresa Barzyk
Concept: G.F.B.

Why Our Status Quo Failed and Is Beyond Reform

Of Two Minds Essentials [sm]

Charles Hugh Smith

Table of Contents

Of Two Minds Essentials^{sm}

Of Two Minds Essentials^{sm} is a collection of short works (30,000 words or less) that address the core issues of our era in distilled form.

Introduction

That our status quo has failed and is beyond reform is self-evident to many, but the idea is far from mainstream. In this book, I will explain why the status quo—the current pyramid of wealth and power dominated by the few at the top—has failed and why the system is beyond reform.

The failure is not rooted in superficial issues such as which political party is in power, or which regulations are enforced; *the failure is structural.* The foundation of the status quo has rotted away, and brushing on another coat of reformist paint will not rebuild the foundation or save the house from collapse.

Though we're assured our status quo offers equal opportunity to all, the reality is *our status quo exists to protect the privileges of the few at the expense of the many.*

Those who benefit from our status quo naturally deny it has failed, for the reason *that it has yet to fail them personally.*

Why can't our status quo be reformed? There are two primary reasons: 1) those benefiting from the current arrangement will resist any reforms that threaten their share of the pie—and any meaningful reforms will necessarily threaten everyone's slice of the pie; and 2) reforms that actually address the structural flaws will bring the system down, as the status quo can only continue if its engine (permanent expansion of debt and consumption) is running at full speed. Once the engine stalls or even slows, the system collapses.

This is unwelcome news to privileged insiders, but it is good news for the planet and everyone else, as the collapse will clear the way for a much more sustainable decentralized system that is already visible to those who know where to look.

This is a topic I have explored in previous books, from *Survival+* in 2009 to *Why Things Are Falling Apart* in 2012. Longtime readers will find familiar material here, but also new system-level advances.

Chapter One

Humanity's Six Integrated Problems

Why has the status quo failed? Let's begin by examining the six great problems facing humanity. These are not six separate problems— they are all aspects of one world-system.

1. Entrenched poverty
2. An economic model of expanding consumption in a world of finite resources
3. An economic model that relies on wages to distribute the output of an economy
4. A political-economic model of centralized banks/states managing economies
5. An economic model that depends on ever-expanding credit, i.e. borrowing from the future, to fund today's consumption
6. A crisis of purpose and meaning

Each problem is complex, and describing each one in depth would require a shelf of books.

But let's keep things simple and describe only the key dynamics of each problem.

We can constructively view these six problems as facets of one central problem: sustainably managing the planet's resources so the basics of prosperity are available to everyone in the global economy. Any real solution to this problem must be a fully integrated—that is, every aspect of the solution must reinforce all the other aspects.

These six problems are generally viewed through the prism of ideologies that were formulated in past eras: Keynesian deficit-spending social-welfare capitalism was developed in the 1920s and 1930s, and Marxism reached maturity in the late 19th and early 20th centuries. The critique of both ideologies posed by the Austrian School of economics was also developed by the mid-20th century.

Regardless of the ideological starting point, Problems 2, 3, 4 and 5 are generally viewed as the solution to Problem 1, entrenched poverty. If consumption expands, so will wages, which lift people out of poverty by providing higher income. The government/ central state (let's simply call it *the state* from now on) alleviates whatever poverty cannot be addressed by rising consumption by taxing profits and wages and redistributing the revenue to the impoverished. In the socialist model, the state owns key enterprises and distributes the profits to alleviate poverty.

Credit is an integral part of growth and state spending. If taxes don't cover state expenditures, the solution is for the state to borrow money by selling bonds. This is known as deficit spending. If private consumption declines, the solution is to lower interest rates and make it easier for people and enterprises to borrow money.

The ideological differences boil down to debates over how best to spur growth of consumption and wages, and what role the state and its central bank play in boosting growth with easier credit.

If these four solutions are now problems in their own right, all the conventional means of addressing poverty will necessarily fail.

How did models that have been widely viewed as solutions become problems? Let's briefly explore each of the six problems.

Entrenched Poverty

We understand entrenched poverty intuitively: it's a poverty that isn't solved with gifts of money or helicopter drops of food. It's a poverty born of systemic inequalities of capital, education and resources. We also intuitively understand that inequality generates poverty. If inequality is rising as a consequence of the way the status quo is structured, the only possible output of the status quo is poverty: not just a poverty of income, but of opportunity to own the sources of wealth, what is known as *capital*.

What is less intuitive is the connection between poverty and the conditions that are widely seen as the causes of poverty: overpopulation, resource depletion and predatory governments (oligarchies, theocracies and kleptocracies). We all understand that having more mouths to feed than the land can support leads to widespread hunger. Decades of birth records have found a direct correlation between birth rates and rising prosperity: as household

4

education and income rates rise, birth rates plummet. So the best way to lower birth rates is alleviate the poverty of households—especially of women.

Poverty actually worsens resource depletion, as the pressure to earn a meager income today pushes the poor to mismanage resources. Global markets distort the value of resources, leading to their exploitation, to the detriment of sustainable production for the local populace.

In other words, poverty is intrinsically wasteful, as the tools, capital and knowledge needed to manage resources productively are as lacking as cash.

The stranglehold that elites have over national economies is a key cause of wide-spread poverty. When we read that one despot siphoned $70 billion out of his impoverished nation, our blood boils when we imagine all the good that could have been done had that money been invested in the local economy rather than being transferred to a Swiss bank account.

It's tempting to think that the way to alleviate poverty is to reduce birth rates, resource depletion and poor governance. But this approach has it backwards: these are as much the results of poverty as its causes. First alleviate poverty, and birth rates will decline, resource management will improve and despotic governance will face newly empowered voices for civil liberties and economic opportunities.

To alleviate entrenched poverty, we first need to identify its primary sources.

Entrenched poverty is characterized by a chronic shortage of the tools needed to create prosperity. These tools include education, best practices (i.e. processes that work sustainably, effectively and predictably), appropriate technologies, productive cultural values, natural resources, transparent marketplaces that foster trade, safe places to live and work and rule of law so disputes are settled in a fair and timely manner.

But all these complex issues obscure the simple truth that the ultimate sources of poverty are a lack of paid work and productive capital that is owned by the many rather than the few. That entrenched poverty results from a lack of paying work and capital may seem so obvious that it barely deserves mention. But if we could re-set the system to generate paid work for everyone who wanted a job and enable the accumulation of capital by every worker, we would have taken the one essential step toward solving all the secondary sources of poverty.

The conventional solution to poverty is economic growth: if the market and the state generate growth of credit and consumption, then this growth will create more jobs, and this expansion of paid work will lift more people out of poverty.

That this idea is no longer working is not just a matter of bad luck or poor execution. Its core solutions—expanding consumption, credit and state power—actively increase poverty rather than alleviate it.

As a result of the inescapable forces of automation, paid labor is in decline everywhere. So even if the state and market boost credit and consumption, this will only speed the collapse of systems that no longer function as they did decades ago.

An Economic Model of Expanding Consumption in a World of Finite Resources

It seems painfully obvious that Planet Earth and its resources are finite. Yet it is only recently in human history that the scale of human consumption has reached the point where vast ecosystems such as the world's oceans are in danger of collapse as a result of human consumption.

The seas offer an instructive example of how our economic ideologies are blind to the concepts of *finite* and *consequence*. Endless growth requires expanding consumption. Conventional economics holds that if we run out of something, then something else can be substituted. Our ideologies assume this process of substitution is infinite, and there will always be a substitute for what we have depleted.

If the seas are stripped of Bluefin tuna, the solution is to catch other kinds of tuna. When all tuna species are exhausted, then we can switch to cod. When the cod are depleted, we can switch to mackerel. And so on, forever.

But we have reached such a large population (seven billion humans) and high rate of consumption that we are stripping the seas of all fish. The conventional economic solution is to create an equivalently vast aquaculture that raises the fish we want to consume in captivity.

But *the natural world is an economy with its own rules*, and imposing our simplistic ideas of substitution doesn't work. Aquaculture turns out to be riddled with pitfalls and problems, and it is not as cheap and easy to raise hundreds of millions of fish in captivity as it was to catch them in the wild.

Conventional economics assumes aquaculture (and everything else) operates as a machine: if we control the inputs and processes, we control the outputs.

The dominant metaphor of industrial civilization is the machine, and we have applied this metaphor to the natural world: if we control the inputs and processes, then we can guarantee the output we desire. This metaphor allows us to believe in endlessly expanding consumption.

But the natural world is an ecosystem, not a machine, and ecosystems operate by different (and more complex) rules than machines. Ecosystems are inherently complex, so controlling a few inputs (food pellets, antibiotics, etc.) does not guarantee factory-like outputs.

Substitutions based on assuming we can make natural systems into machines fail for intrinsic reasons: fish don't thrive just on food pellets and antibiotics; they require a complex ecosystem.

We can extend this basic insight to human economies: conventional economics assume controlling inputs (interest rates, credit, etc.) will yield the desired output (permanent growth). But these mechanistic models have failed, for the reason that economies and societies are ecosystems, not simplistic machines.

As for commodities like oil, copper and iron ore that we extract from the Earth: while there is plenty left, what's left is deep in the ground or dispersed and therefore increasingly costly to extract.

It is widely recognized that industrial society stagnates when the cost of oil skyrockets. There is nothing mysterious about this. Spending more on energy leaves less in the household budget to spend on other things, or invest in some productive use. As consumption and investment both plummet, the economy stagnates.

Even though there may be resources in the ground, it does not follow that it makes economic sense to extract them if the cost is high. And if the cost climbs enough to justify extraction, the ripple effect of those high costs undermines the very growth that the resources are supposed to fuel.

Humans are designed to solve local depletion of resources by moving on. This has been the solution for tens of thousands of years, and it is one reason why humans have filled every niche from the Arctic to the Amazon.

For the first time in human history, moving to a new locale is no longer a solution. There is no place left to move to.

Fossil fuels have given humanity an immense pool of *energy slaves* that we use to do work that is beyond mere human muscle. This has fostered the illusion that there are no limits on our consumption: cheap energy has fostered a belief that we can always build more machines to generate more energy, food, fresh water, etc.

Cheap fossil fuels have enabled the expansion of inefficient and wasteful systems such as centralized bureaucracies and the ideology of consumerism. These systems appear affordable and sustainable because the energy needed to fuel them is cheap. Once energy is expensive/ in short supply, these foundations of the status quo no longer make financial sense.

As I write this in mid-2016, energy is once again relatively inexpensive: the world is awash in oil, and natural gas and coal prices are low. Technological innovations such as fracking, and cheap credit to fund the expansion of energy production, have led to a surplus of energy that has pushed the price down.

But this doesn't change the fact that the oil that was the cheapest to pump and refine has been depleted, leaving the future only the oil that is more costly to pump and refine. The current era of low energy costs will end, as demand soars when prices are low (we waste what is cheap and conserve what is dear) and expanding production depletes what is left of the cheap-to-access oil.

In effect, the status quo needs cheap energy to function. The era of financialization, particularly the 2009-2016 period of sustained central bank manipulation of global finances, has fed the illusion that printing

8

money and creating limitless credit will magically fuel the endless expansion of energy supplies.

Unlike the world of digital banking, in which money can be created in limitless quantities by a few keystrokes in a central bank, energy is in the real world. Central banks can print limitless sums of money, but they can't print limitless amounts of energy, phosphate, lithium, wild fish, etc. at prices low enough to sustain the wasteful and over-indebted status quo.

Making use of appropriate technology offers a sustainable future, but sustainability does not mean endless expansion of consumption. Endless expansion of consumption is based on two compelling illusions: everything that we deplete has a substitute, and the natural world is a machine that we can easily manipulate, given enough free money, to produce more of everything we consume.

The status quo model that makes expanding consumption the foundation of prosperity is failing for profoundly systemic reasons. It is failing because its assumptions—cheap substitutes are always available, cheap energy is limitless and machines can solve any shortage—have intrinsic limits.

This reality deeply offends many people because it violates their core belief in *no limits*. There are no limits on the expansion of credit and money issued by central banks, but there are limits in the finite real world.

An Economic Model that Uses Wages to Distribute the Output of the Economy

Author Jeremy Rifkin identified the consequence of automation technologies in his book, *The End of Work*: increasing swaths of human labor are being replaced by software and machines.

The replacement of human labor by machines is a trend that has been in place for centuries. Each wave of technological advancement destroyed jobs but created opportunities for even more employment, generally in service industries.

This leads many to believe the trend of technology creating more employment than it destroys is as permanent as technological advancement itself. But the trend of technology expanding employment has reversed for two reasons:

1. Digital communications and processing technology is rapidly replacing service sector jobs and higher-skill jobs that were widely assumed to be irreplaceable by machines.

2. The number of new jobs created by the rise of digital software is dwarfed by the number of jobs being lost.

It only takes a handful of programmers a relatively short time to program software that replaces thousands of service jobs. The tremendous leverage of digital technologies has yet to be fully realized; those closest to the technologies see no end to the trend of software and machines replacing human labor.

For example, CraigsList's 50-plus employees eliminated tens of thousands of classified and print-media jobs.

3. As costs of human labor rise globally, employers have ever-greater financial incentives to replace human labor with software and robots.

Socio-economist Immanuel Wallerstein identified the key drivers of higher labor costs, not just in developed nations but in all economies:

1. Urbanization of the global populace (wages are higher in urban zones)

2. The external costs of industrialization coming due (mitigating pollution, unsafe water, etc.)

3. The rising costs of labor overhead (pensions, healthcare, disability insurance, etc.)

4. The rising demands on the state for more social spending

In developed economies, labor overhead expenses can easily exceed workers' salaries. In developing economies, the external costs of polluted water, air and soil fall on the economy as a whole, and as a result costs rise—not just for goods and services but for labor as well.

As demands for the state to spend more money on education, healthcare and pensions increase, taxes must rise. Regardless of the type of taxation—on wages, consumption or capital—higher taxes increase the incentives to replace human labor with technology, as private enterprise has few other ways to offset higher costs.

The prime directive of capitalism is the accumulation of capital: enterprises that fail to accumulate capital go bust. As economist Joseph

Schumpeter recognized, capitalism is not a steady-state system but one constantly reworked by *creative destruction*, the process of the less efficient being replaced by the more efficient.

This is as true of socialist-owned enterprises as it is of private enterprises. Companies that fail to make a profit and reinvest some of that profit in new capacities lose money and go bankrupt. Socialist owners can subsidize losing companies with tax revenues, but this diverts money that could have been invested productively into a dead-end. This saps the vitality of the economy and the socialist system slides into insolvency.

Many assume that the companies replacing humans with machines will grow increasingly profitable as a result of cutting expenses. But as the cost of software and robotics declines, the barriers to competition are lowered: if you can buy cheap software and robots, so can your competitors. As a result, profits shrink as automation becomes a *commodity*, i.e. something that can be made anywhere by anyone. Software and robots can work anywhere producing the same goods and services; products, places and companies are all interchangeable.

In this environment, capital is no longer able to reap big profits, and companies will be under even more financial pressure to lower costs by replacing human labor with automation. In effect, declining profits act as a driver for further reductions of labor, speeding up the replacement of human workers with robots and software.

As Wallerstein observed, the state depends on corporations reaping substantial profits to fund its own spending. The structural decline of profits is not a temporary phenomenon—it is a permanent feature of the current version of global capitalism, what Wallerstein calls a *world-system*.

Wallerstein's chapter in the recent book *Does Capitalism Have a Future?* (Oxford University Press, 2013) is titled *why capitalists may no longer find capitalism rewarding*.

Since the state depends on substantial private-sector profits for its funding, the erosion of profits means the state will also be starved of funding. Those who place their faith in the state funding permanent employment for all forget the state generates no surplus—it needs profits and wages to tax.

11

If both wages and profits are in permanent decline, so too are state revenues.

This leads to a sobering conclusion: wages are no longer an adequate means for distributing a nation's income. Those counting on immense corporate profits to fund social welfare for everyone without a job (often called *Universal Basic Income*) will be as disappointed as those expecting technology to create more jobs.

The trend of increasingly costly human labor being replaced by technology will not fade; rather, it will gain momentum. The declining cost and advancing capabilities of automation will hollow out profits rather than boost profits.

Neither of the current models—wages and social welfare—will survive automation. In effect, labor, profits and the state are being squeezed by unprecedented technological advancements.

We can easily see this erosion of jobs in the U.S. data. Full-time jobs in the U.S. declined from 121 million in 2007 to 119 million in 2014, while the working age population rose by 16 million. The population of working-age without any paid work is over 94 million. Out of roughly 250 million people who are of working age, less than half have full-time employment—and 21 million of these work for the government, which funds their paychecks by taxing the 98 million private-sector workers and their employers.

To understand the full import of these figures, we need to recall that the U.S. economy has been expanding for seven years, and the federal government and central Bank (Federal Reserve) have pursued unprecedented fiscal deficits and monetary expansion to stimulate the economy since 2008.

Despite an excess of the inputs conventional economists expected to generate the desired output of higher employment, the reality is there are fewer full-time jobs than before the state and central bank pursued their policy extremes.

Clearly, the status quo policies of deficit spending and monetary stimulus have failed.

A Political-Economic Model of Central States Dominated by Elites

Daron Acemoglu and James A. Robinson demonstrated in their book *Why Nations Fail* that economies organized to benefit elites at the expense of everyone else trap the vast majority of people in poverty.

Rising inequality is the *ontological imperative* of elite-dominated economies: there is no other possible result of elite-dominated economies other than rising inequality and poverty.

(*Ontology* is a word used in philosophy to describe the core features and dynamics of a concept or entity: ontology describes why it cannot be anything other than what it is. An *ontological imperative* is the core directive of system, what it must do by its very nature.)

The mechanism is starkly visible in corrupt economies where elites and the *Upper Caste* (also called the *Clerisy class*) of technocrats that serve the elites control all the centers of power: finance, the military, police, judiciary, media and the core assets of wealth creation: factories, mines, railroads, shipping, etc.

In these economies, the mechanics of democracy may be acted out for public-relations purposes. Beneath the façade of false choices and bribed voters, the political machinery is still ruled by elites.

Any group that attempts to wrest power away from the elites and their Upper Caste of technocrats is ruthlessly suppressed or marginalized.

This is the primary reason why inequality and poverty have remained entrenched in so much of the world: it is impractical for the powerless to wrest power from elites who are adept at bribing key constituencies, shaping opinion with mass media and suppressing dissent with police or military force.

Centralization of power is a necessary feature of these elite-dominated societies and economies. Elites cannot organize economies to benefit themselves at the expense of everyone else without centralized power. Centralization is the leverage elites need to establish and maintain control of the nation's income and wealth.

Acemoglu and Robinson identify the rise of non-elite institutions as the key feature of liberal democracies that enabled the expansion of a middle class. The incentives created by these institutions shape the prosperity of the nation. Exploitive institutions do not offer people the incentives to save, invest, take risks and innovate. Constructive institutions create incentives for the foundation of widespread prosperity: savings, investing, long-term planning, risk-taking and innovation.

Unfortunately, centralized, hierarchical institutions fail for three reasons:

1. Those laboring within the institution focus on serving their own interests, eroding the core purpose of the institution.

2. Elites gain control of the institution via concentrated financial and political power.

3. Institutions reward *process (following the rules)* rather than *outcomes*, in effect rewarding failure.

The *ontology of institutions* is to dissipate accountability, suppress transparency and increase the income and power of insiders at the expense of those outside the institution. The dissipation of accountability protects the individuals within institutions from the consequences of failure. The suppression of transparency protects individuals from criticism. Expanding the income and power of those within to increase their pensions and perquisites and protect those gains.

Ironically, the impulse to institutionalize accountability to limit self-interest creates layers of bureaucracy that add to the cost of maintaining the institution, leaving fewer resources to pursue its core purpose. We see this in colleges and universities, which have added tens of thousands of highly paid administrative staff while slashing the number of professors in classrooms.

A more subtle erosion undermines the system as navigating bureaucratic complexities becomes the most valuable skillset of managers. As managers who excel at protecting the institution's power advance up the management ladder, they leave those who excel at the core purpose in lesser positions.

Institutions hollowed out by these forces are increasingly vulnerable to self-interest and elite influence. As self-preservation trumps purpose, institutional leadership is easily co-opted by powerful elites.

The end result is an institution bent on self-preservation at all costs, an institution that is failing at its core purpose but is incapable of reforming itself.

As noted above, higher education has been hollowed out from within by a self-serving Clerisy class. This erosion of purpose has enabled powerful elites to profit from the trillion dollar student loan system that has emerged to fund the institutions.

Higher education has eroded to the point that there is no accountability for its failure to prepare students for the real economy. A recent major study, *Academically Adrift: Limited Learning on College Campuses*, concluded that *"American higher education is characterized by limited or no learning for a large proportion of students."*

While student loans have soared to over $1.2 trillion, with direct Federal loans ballooning from $115 billion to over $700 billion in a few short years, only 37% of freshmen at four-year colleges graduate in four years (58% finally graduate in six years), and 53% of recent college graduates under the age of 25 are unemployed or doing work they could have done without going to college.

This is total systemic failure. Yet the Clerisy class running the institutions claims all is well. A recent essay, *Higher Education's Aristocrats*, noted that "Over five years, (university) administrators enjoyed pay increases of between 40 percent and 135 percent, and as a result each received $450,000 to $3.3 million from cumulative increases by the end of 2012-2013, the most recent year for which tax data is available."

Meanwhile, the financial institutions that control the more than $1 trillion in student loans have created a vast class of student *debt-serfs* who must pay interest on their loans for much of their productive lives or face harsh penalties imposed by a political system that serves financial elites.

Marginal learning, abysmal graduation rates, soaring costs, self-serving insiders enriching themselves at the expense of students burdened with crushing debt and unprepared for the real economy—this is a thoroughly corrupt system in which institutions have lost their way but retain expertise in enriching insiders.

The failure of advanced liberal democratic economies is the direct result of three dynamics which are visible in the example of higher education. These dynamics are not limited to one sector; they are systemic, meaning that they are present throughout advanced economies.

1. Financialization
2. State dependence on private-sector profits from financialization for revenues
3. Enriching elites under the guise of broadening opportunity

Definitions of financialization vary, but the basic process is the transformation of low-risk, low-profit debt into high-risk, high-profit speculation that enriches the financial sector and state at the expense of other sectors of the economy.

Financialization introduces perverse incentives that distort and corrupt the economy. The huge profits to be reaped from financializing debt leads households and enterprises alike to engage in highly risky speculation and to over-invest in speculation at the expense of lower-risk, more productive investments.

My definition of financialization is:

Financialization is the mass commodification of debt and debt-based financial instruments collaterized by previously low-risk assets, a pyramiding of risk and speculative gains that is only possible in a massive expansion of credit and leverage.

Another way to describe the same dynamic is: *financialization results when leverage and information asymmetry replace innovation and productive investment as the source of wealth creation.*

When the profits from financializing collateral and leveraging those bets far exceeds the income from creating products and services, the economy is soon hollowed out as the perverse incentives of financialization start driving business decisions and strategies.

The elimination of low-risk interest income in favor of speculative asset bubbles leads to a monumental misallocation of capital and the institutionalization of perverse incentives. Financialization effectively drains low-risk income from households and forces savers onto the tilted game board of risky speculation—a game the average wage-earner is unlikely to win, especially when critical information about risk is kept secret by the financial heavyweights who control the game. This *information asymmetry* is the equivalent of a rigged card game or roulette wheel: the players are assured the game is equally risky to everyone, but insiders reap all the gains at the expense of those who don't know the game is rigged.

Why is financialization so destructive? It's actually very simple: when debt-fueled speculative profits outpace economic growth, the rich get richer, increasing inequality.

Home mortgages once operated as a financial utility: banks issued low-risk mortgages and held the loans to maturation. Financialization transformed this low-risk investment into a highly risky speculation by bundling mortgages into pools that were then divided into tranches and sold to investors as "safe" securities.

Financialization claims to increase profits at near-zero risk, but this is an illusion: enormous profits arise from enormous risks, and the process of financialization purposely masks those risks to sell risky securities to unwary investors.

Higher education is a good example of financialization at work. Rather than innovate to bring costs down to what student can afford, higher education addressed its soaring costs by financializing the cost of attending university. Student loans are packaged into securities and sold to investors (or the government) as low-risk investments.

What makes loans to students with little or no income low-risk? The state promises to extract payments from the students regardless of their poverty.

This highlights the state's partnership with financial elites. Now that the risks of student loans defaulting is unavoidable, the state has stepped in and bought most of the student loan debt from private lenders, transferring the risk to taxpayers while leaving the profits in private hands.

This should not surprise us, for as noted earlier, the state depends on private-sector wages and profits for its own funding. As technology and global competition erode profits, the enormous profits of financialization become the foundation of state funding.

A generation ago, the financial sector generated less than 10% of U.S. corporate profits. Now finance reaps over 30% of all profits. Indeed, many corporations earn more from loans and finance than from their core businesses.

Engorged with tax revenues from these speculative windfalls, the state increases its spending. As a result, the state has become dependent on financialization for its own funding. The state and central bank have institutionalized the speculative excesses of financialization to further their own power at the expense of the majority whose wealth and income have been strip-mined by financialization.

Wallerstein is one of the few who clearly understands the state's role as enforcer of profitable monopolies and cartels. In an era of declining returns on capital, the state needs secure profits to fund its own revenues. High profit margins are best maintained by the state protecting quasi-monopolies and cartels from competition.

If the state fails to maintain cartels, profit margins plummet. In other words, the state isn't a passive patsy in financialization—it is a willing partner, because financialization funds the state. As evidence, consider the enormous expansion of property taxes and income taxes that flowed from the housing and stock market bubbles.

This is why Wallerstein characterizes the current world-system as "a particular historical configuration of *markets and state structures* where private economic gain by almost any means is the paramount goal and measure of success."

Financialization is a process that concentrates wealth and corrupts institutions such as home mortgages and higher education. As profits from goods and services erode, the state reinforces the concentration of wealth and power as the only available means of securing its own revenues.

Neoliberalism—the liberalizing of the economy by relaxing regulatory controls and opening markets to competition—plays a dual role. When neoliberal policies replace elite-controlled institutions with opportunities that are accessible to the majority, these are broadly constructive.

The classic example of liberalization is land reform that breaks up feudal estates into small private farm plots. Freed from the onerous crop-sharing arrangement enforced by the feudal lord, the peasants become more productive and get to keep most of their gains in productivity.

This is the basic promise of neoliberalism: by loosening the grip of elites and the state, opportunities are opened for everyone who had been trapped in servitude to elites.

But this is only half the story of neoliberalism. In advanced economies, neoliberal policies may not replace elites with broad-based opportunities for all—the policies simply substitute new elites for the old ones.

A classic example is control of a town's water supply. Neoliberal policies call for municipally owned water utilities to be sold off, on the promise that private firms will lower costs as competition will be encouraged.

Yet the outcome of neoliberalism is the water utility is bought by a global corporation that then raises prices because it is a monopoly—there are no other suppliers of water in town. The existing elite (the managers of the municipally owned water company) has simply been replaced by a new elite (the corporation) that is focused solely on increasing private profits at the expense of the citizenry.

The citizens are worse off in two ways: more of their wealth is extracted by the corporation, and they have far less influence over the corporation than they did over the municipal water utility.

Neoliberalism is constructive when it replaces elite-controlled systems with broad-based opportunities accessible to all. But it is destructive when it simply replaces existing elites with new elites.

If we understand the state needs private enterprise to earn substantial profits for the state to increase its own spending, we understand why the state partners with private elites. We also understand why the modern state/central bank actively encourages risky, speculative financialization: though it is terribly destructive, financialization is the only mechanism left that generates the profits needed to prop up state revenues.

This is the end-game of economies managed by central states and banks: highly destructive financial dynamics are encouraged as the only short-term way left to fund the state and keep the economy from faltering. The terrible irony is that neoliberal financialization concentrates wealth and power in the hands of elites and pushes the state into a destructive dependence on risky debt-fueled speculation.

There is no possible outcome of this system other than collapse, as speculative bubbles fueled by ever-rising debt always implode, destroying all participants.

Now that the state is dependent on the profits reaped by speculative bubbles and ever-rising debt, when the bubble pops, it won't just be the financial sector that implodes—the state itself will fail as well.

As we shall see in the next chapter, the way the status quo creates and distributes money insures that wealth becomes concentrated in the hands of the few, who then have the means to buy influence over the concentrated power of the state. Once this arrangement takes hold, democracy dies. This is the status quo in a nutshell.

An Economic Model that Depends on Credit (Borrowing from the Future) to Fund Today's Consumption

Nations everywhere face a quandary. With growth slowing due to global competition, automation and the perverse incentives of financialization, the state's revenues are stagnating even as citizens demand more social spending.

In response, the State raises taxes and borrows the difference between its spending and its revenues. Higher taxes crimp investment and household consumption, further weakening the economy. The deficit spending increases the debt and the interest the state must pay, squeezing other state spending.

Borrowing from the future to pay for consumption today creates a destructive, self-reinforcing feedback loop: the more the state taxes and borrows, the more it weakens the economy. Raising taxes weakens the investment needed to expand the economy, and the rising cost of debt service is an ever-tightening noose around state spending.

Borrowing money is productive if the capital is invested in uses that yield a higher return than the cost of the borrowing. When developing economies are starved for cash to invest in highly productive investments such as railways, expanding credit works wonders because the resulting growth in income and assets dwarfs the cost of borrowing.

A common analogy is plucking the low-hanging fruit from a tree. In an economy starved of cash and credit, investments in canals, roads, railways, electrical generation, etc. generate huge returns on the initial capital because the infrastructure enables a vast expansion of

20

secondary activity: with transportation and electricity available to all, private enterprise expands rapidly

This scenario is ideal for the state, as growth outpaces the cost of deficits. The state can continue to borrow freely, confident that tax revenues from the expanding economy will outpace the cost of borrowing.

But eventually the low-hanging fruit is all plucked, and high-yield investments become scarce. This exhaustion of high-yield investments characterize developed economies. In developed consumer economies, corporations find it more profitable to buy back their own stock rather than invest in new goods and services.

In response, the central bank lowers the cost of borrowing and floods the economy with credit, in the hopes that borrowing will pick up. Ironically, this flood of cheap credit does nothing to expand productive investments. All it does is create incentives to borrow money for speculation.

As the rate of investment declines, state revenues no longer expand faster than the state's borrowing costs. State borrowing becomes a burden, as the cost of servicing debt (i.e. the interest payments) crowds out other spending.

Central banks have come up with the financial equivalent of the perpetual motion machine to enable more state borrowing. The central bank creates money out of thin air and uses this cash to buy government bonds. The bonds go on the bank balance sheet as interest-earning assets, and the state gets the cash to spend.

But these tricks cannot change the core truth that borrowing money to fund today's consumption is borrowing from future taxpayers, who must continue to pay interest on the debt for their entire lives. This takes income from the future and spends it today.

The problem is that the gap between the state's obligations and its revenues widens every year due to demographics (a declining work force supporting a larger population of retirees), declining employment and stagnating profits on real-world goods and services.

The central bank's last-ditch fix—institutionalizing financialization to generate high profits—hollows out the real economy and incentivizes the very excesses of debt and speculation that insure failure of the entire status quo.

21

The declining returns on expanding debt is *scale-invariant*, meaning that it operates not just in large economies but in household budgets. The first pair of shoes a shoeless consumer buys provides enormous benefits. Borrowing a bit of money to buy the first pair of shoes offers a big return on the investment.

The fifth pair of shoes the consumer buys offers far less value, and there is an *opportunity cost* to the purchase: what else could have been purchased with the same money that would provide a much higher return than the superfluous shoes?

This example characterizes the consumer-driven advanced economies: the vast majority of people have everything necessary for basic well-being, and the majority has a surplus of food, clothing, entertainment, etc.

In response to this satiation, the consumerist economy tempts consumers to borrow money to make impulse buys or chase fads and fashions. This reliance on consumerism leads to what I call *permanent adolescence*—the impulsive state of mind of an insecure teen with a credit card and a keen desire to establish a high-status identity by buying stuff.

So not only is the status quo's borrowing from the future to fund today's consumption bankrupt—so is the strategy of stimulating excess consumption with cheap credit. The destructiveness of financialization is paralleled by the psychological destructiveness of *permanent adolescence*.

Just as the teen falls into depression when the credit card has been exhausted and the bills come due, nations encounter an equivalent financial and social black hole when they borrow from the future to fund today's consumption.

A Crisis of Purpose and Meaning

The causal connection between material well-being and happiness is both obvious and complex. We cannot be happy if we're hungry, cold and scared. But once these basic needs have been satisfied, the correlation between material wealth and happiness frays. It turns out that additional material wealth adds little to happiness. Happiness and

22

fulfillment are highly correlated to purpose, shared goals, meaningful work, a secure place in society and a circle of friends and collaborators.

Two key characteristics of the status quo are at odds with these sources of happiness and fulfillment: the ideology of consumerism, which promises the more we buy, the happier we will be, and the social welfare system of the state, which eliminates the social and economic layers between the recipient and the state itself.

In other words, the recipient of social welfare has no need to be productive in a community, workplace or social circle; the money comes directly from the state.

The state payments enable consumption, but offer no source of purpose, shared goals, meaningful work or a *positive social role in the community*. The status quo strips the welfare recipient of positive incentives and fosters an unhealthy dependence on the state—a dependence that is nothing but a modern form of serfdom.

The failure of rising consumption and social welfare is not just in what they don't provide; both undermine the foundations of human happiness and fulfillment. Consumerism and dependency on the state create *social defeat*.

In my lexicon, *social defeat* is the spectrum of anxiety, insecurity, chronic stress, powerlessness, and fear of declining social status.

A status quo that excels in creating and distributing social defeat will be populated with unhappy, depressed, anxious, and frustrated people, regardless of the material prosperity they possess.

One aspect of social defeat is the emptiness we experience when prosperity does not deliver the promised sense of fulfillment. A recent sociological study compared wealthy Hong Kong residents' sense of contentment with those of the poorly-paid immigrant maids who serve the moneyed Elites. The study found that the maids were much happier than their wealthy masters, who were often suicidal and depressed. The maids, on the other hand, had a trustworthy group – other maids they met with on their one day off – and the purpose of providing financial support for their families back home.

It is widely agreed that China's rise to prosperity is among the greatest expansion of material wealth in human history. Yet China's people are experiencing not rising happiness and fulfillment but a sense of spiritual emptiness and psychological anxiety that are fueling an equally dramatic expansion of religious faiths in China.

The loss of purpose, meaning, positive social roles and community are not unique to any one nation or culture; they are manifesting across the globe, despite rising wealth and material well-being.

Is the Status Quo Solving These Problems, Or Is It the Problem?

The status quo is not only failing to solve humanity's six critical problems—*the status quo is itself the problem*.

Let's review the six problems and ask, *is the status quo solving this problem or is it creating the problem?*

1. Entrenched poverty: as we shall see in Chapter Two, *the way the status quo creates and distributes money insures rising inequality and poverty: the status quo is the problem.*

2. An economic model of expanding consumption in a world of finite resources: *the status quo is based on this model, so it is the problem.*

3. An economic model that relies on wages to distribute the output of an economy: the status quo is based on rising wages and profits, and has no solution to declining wages and profits. *The status quo is the problem.*

4. A political-economic model of centralized banks/states managing economies: The concentration of wealth and power undermine social mobility and democracy. *The status quo is the problem.*

5. An economic model that depends on ever-expanding credit, i.e. borrowing from the future, to fund today's consumption. The status quo depends on borrowing from the future to fund today's consumption, so *it is the problem.*

6. A crisis of purpose and meaning: the status quo depends on consumerism and social welfare. Consumerism is devoid of purpose and meaning and universal basic income (Welfare for All) is nothing but a system for distributing social defeat and modern-day serfdom: *the status quo is the source of this problem.*

The status quo is not just failing to solve the six problems—it is the source of the problems. The only way to solve these problems is to create an alternative system with entirely different foundations, values and processes.

Chapter Two

How Money Is Created and Distributed

The way the status quo creates and distributes money is the root of inequality and poverty.

The status quo has three mechanisms for creating money. One is the central bank creates money out of thin air and either loans the money to private banks or uses it to buys bonds.

In either case, the loans or bonds are entered as assets on the central bank's balance sheet. If the central bank creates $1 million (no need to actually print $1 million in bills; the central bank creates digital money with a keyboard), the liability of $1 million is offset by the $1 million asset of the bond or the interest-bearing loan.

The second mechanism is the state's Treasury prints paper money and uses it to pay the state's obligations: pensions, payrolls, payments for goods, etc.

There are key differences between the two mechanisms. In the first case, the loan or bond that the central bank owns is self-liquidating, meaning that once the borrower redeems the bond at maturity, the liability is erased. The money that was created out of thin air—the liability—is zeroed out as the loan is paid off or the bond is redeemed.

The loan that was issued or the bond that was purchased is a marketable asset, meaning that it could in theory be sold in the open market to another buyer. The value of the central bank's assets is established by the marketplace for loans and bonds. In other words, the value of the asset is not just a matter of the central bank's word—in theory, the value of the bank's assets is established (we can also say *discovered*) by a transparent market of buyers and sellers.

In the second case, the newly issued money isn't backed by any marketable asset. The value of the new money—that is, its *purchasing power*, or how many goods and services it can buy—is ultimately set by the relative *scarcity* of the paper currency. If demand for the paper money exceeds the supply, the value of the currency will rise. If the supply of paper currency exceeds the demand for the money, its value (purchasing power) will decline.

This decline in the purchasing power of money is what we call *inflation*: money buys less than it did in the past. An extreme example shows how the purchasing power of a nation's currency can be destroyed by the uncontrolled issuance of new money.

Let's say the government decides to pay everyone $1 million per hour. The amount of goods and services will not expand; only the number of dollars chasing the available goods and services will expand.

Let's say that the average hourly wage can buy four loaves of bread. Very quickly, the cost of four loaves of bread will rise to $1 million—the pay for one hour's work.

Measured in what an hour of labor can buy, nothing has changed. But whatever cash people had before the hourly wage went to $1 million has instantly become worthless. $1 million—a lifetime's earnings in today's economy—would be reduced to the cash equivalent of four loaves of bread.

This is known as *hyper-inflation*, and history offers many examples that prove that hyper-inflation results when states print money with abandon.

Compare this with the central bank model, where the new money is offset by self-liquidating assets. It's clear why this model has endured; new money can be sustainably created and injected into the economy in two ways:

1. The state sells bonds to the central bank and spends the money on payrolls, pensions, etc. This injects the newly created money into the economy.

2. The central bank loans new money to banks which then lend the money to home buyers, businesses, etc. This also injects the new money into the economy.

The third way of creating money is called *fractional reserve lending* by private banks. If a bank has $100 in cash deposits, it can issue a loan for $1000: the bank is allowed to leverage its reserves 10 to 1. (In many cases, the leverage is 15 to 1, 20 to 1, or even higher.) The $900 above and beyond the cash deposit of $100 is new money that is injected into the economy.

The intrinsic problem with fractional reserve lending is that this leverage leaves the bank extremely vulnerable to insolvency. If a bank loans $100 based on $5 in deposits, a $6 loss in its loan portfolio wipes out its reserves: the bank is insolvent.

There are three important dynamics in this process of injecting new money into the economy.

One is that simply creating the money does not mean it will necessarily flow into the economy. It might sit in banks' reserves rather than being issued as new loans. In this case, the new money does not move into the real economy.

The second dynamic is that the new money must increase the *money supply* to enter the real economy. Money created by the central bank that sits in the central bank doesn't enter the money supply, which is the currency, savings and bank accounts held by the public; it just sits there in the central bank doing nothing.

The third point is that brisk economic activity is characterized by a high *money velocity*, which measures how fast money circulates from one transaction to the next.

An example making the rounds of the Internet tells the story of how a single $100 bill moving quickly from hand to hand in a town can soon pay off a mountain of debt one transaction at a time. The velocity of that one $100 bill was high, as the money moved quickly from one transaction to the next. As a result, a great deal of economic activity was enabled by that relatively small sum of money.

The key point here is that there is a critical difference between printing money and injecting it into the economy, and another critical difference between getting the money into the money supply (i.e. the banks and the public's bank accounts) and putting that money into circulation.

In other words, if the money is pushed into the public's accounts but it is left in coffee cans buried in the backyard, it won't circulate. It is *dead money*, just as money sitting in the banks' reserves is dead money.

There is another critical difference between printing paper money and creating *credit money* in a central bank: the interest that must be paid on loans and bonds acts as a form of discipline on the system.

There is no financial limit on how much money can be printed by a Treasury, but the interest on loans and bonds places a financial limit on how much more money can be borrowed. If income has been stretched to the limit by the monthly interest payments on previous borrowing, we cannot borrow more even if we wanted to.

In other words, even if the central bank creates money to encourage bank lending, if households and enterprises have no need or ability to borrow more money, then banks will not be able to create new money by issuing new loans.

If a government borrows profligately, the interest that must be paid on the accumulated debt will eventually crowd out other state spending. To maintain its spending, the state will eventually be tempted to pay the rising interest with more borrowed money. From this point on, a destructive feedback takes hold: higher debt leads to higher interest costs which lead to more debt, and eventually the state defaults on its debts.

No matter which method of money-printing the status quo uses, the end result is inequality: rising wealth for the few and increasing poverty for the many.

Why is this so?

In the status quo, *all money is created and distributed at the top of the power/wealth pyramid*—by central banks, the Treasury and private banks. The only way anyone in the bottom 99.5% of the pyramid can get any of this new money is to borrow it from a bank at a high rate of interest.

Only the wealthy and powerful have access to the nearly free money issued by central banks. The financial Aristocracy can borrow essentially limitless amounts of money at 1% and use it to:

1. Buy assets elsewhere in the world yielding 5% or more, a practice called the *carry trade*
2. Buy back corporate stocks, pushing stock prices higher and reaping billions of dollars in profits
3. Outbid everyone without access to the central bank's nearly free money for income-producing assets such as rental housing
4. Loan money to students, people buying auto and homes or charging purchases on credit cards, etc. at rates that that are as high as 10% or even 20%.

No one in the bottom 99.5% of the wealth/power pyramid can borrow money for 1% and then use the money to lock in immense profits.

If money is created and distributed at the top of the wealth/power pyramid, the only possible result is the rich get richer because they can use the nearly free money to buy wealth-generating assets, and everyone else gets poorer because the only way they can access new money is to borrow it at high rates of interest.

No one paying high rates of interest can compete with financiers paying almost nothing for new money. This is why the *only possible result of the status quo is rising wealth inequality and poverty.*

The Way We Create Money Creates Inequality/Poverty

In the status quo, the money flows to the wealthy, not the poor. Why is this so?

Central banks and Treasuries are political institutions, and as a result the flow of new money is ultimately a political process that is influenced by concentrations of private power and wealth. New money flows to those closest to the money spigot, and the wealthy and powerful position themselves next to the new money spigot.

For example, the state sells bonds as an alternative to raising revenues from taxes. Borrowing money by selling bonds has little negative impact on current taxpayers; the vast majority of the interest expense will be paid by taxpayers in the future, many of whom have yet to be born.

The state will naturally spend this new money satisfying powerful constituencies who influence politicians via campaign contributions and lobbying.

When the central bank creates money and lends it at low rates to private banks, it is in essence handing the wealthy low-cost money to lend at high profit margins or use for speculation.

In other words, the central bank doesn't lend money at near-zero interest rates to households; it lends the money to *extreme concentrations of financial wealth and power at the top of the wealth/power pyramid.*

30

Though central banks claim to be above the political fray, private interests can influence the distribution of the central bank-issued credit money with relatively modest sums of lobbying.

This is the foundation of *centralized money issuance*. If the issuance of money is centralized, a relatively few people control the spigot. Anyone who can influence these few policymakers gains leverage over the money being issued.

The wealthy buy political influence to position themselves next to the central bank money spigot. They have a monopoly on all new money, which flows only to private banks and financiers. No one below the financial Aristocracy gets a single dollar of the new money.

If the system creates and distributes money only at the top of the pyramid, the rich get richer and everyone else becomes poorer as all the income-producing assets end up in the hands of the wealthy.

What if money was created and distributed only in the bottom of the pyramid, rather than only at the top of the pyramid? What if banks and financiers could not get any of the new money?

The power and wealth would shift from the .5% at the apex of the pyramid to the 99.5% in the bottom of the pyramid.

This is why I say: *if we don't change the way we create and distribute money, we change nothing.*

This raises the question: why would the wealthy and powerful allow the source of their wealth and power to slip from their grasp? The answer is of course: they won't.

The Illusory Promise of the Gold Standard

Many people look at the problems that arise from the central bank/state creation of money and conclude that a return to a gold standard would solve these problems.

In a gold standard, the central bank explicitly ties the money it creates to the gold in its vaults. In a simple example, if a central bank owned 1,000 ounces of gold and printed 1,000 paper bills, each bill would have the value of one ounce of gold.

But no monetary system is without drawbacks. In the early 1500s before the Spanish conquest brought the Americas' enormous supply of gold and silver to Europe, gold and silver were in short supply. There simply wasn't enough gold and silver to grease trade transactions. In response, credit money became common: letters of credit or promissory notes, where one merchant issued another merchant a promise to settle a bill at the next trading fair. At the fair, the promissory notes were exchanged in lieu of scarce gold and silver to settle accounts.

In this way, a great many transactions could be settled with very little gold or silver actually changing hands.

Another problem that arises when gold and silver are the only money is the wealthy end up with the vast majority of the gold and silver. Average people need goods and services to maintain their well-being, and so holding gold and silver rather than spending it on goods and services such as food and clothing is not an option.

The wealthy—by definition, those who own income-generating assets such as loans, farmland rented to tenant farmers, and what Karl Marx called the *means of production*—mines, factories, ships, etc.— have a surplus of money beyond what they need for their own survival.

As a result, they accumulate all the gold and silver from those who need goods and services.

Gold-backed money certainly limits inflation (unless of course an influx of new gold or silver enters the economy, increasing the money supply while doing nothing to increase goods and services), but it does not eliminate the practical value of credit-money or address the root causes of poverty.

The Limits of Blockchain Crypto-Currencies

A new decentralized mechanism for creating money has recently been introduced by crypto-currencies such as Bitcoin. These currencies are based on a digital technology called the *blockchain*, which generates a data base for each transaction that enables third parties (also called peer-to-peer) to trust their transactions without a centralized authority such as a bank verifying the transaction.

These currencies have created a new way to create money that is outside the control of the state and central bank. As a result, they are a new form of *symbolic capital*.

The problem with these digital currencies is they are untethered from any source of value other than scarcity. In the bitcoin realm, digital coins are "mined" by software, and their value is based on supply and demand: the supply is limited by design, so the demand sets the purchasing power of the digital coins.

As with conventional money systems, the wealthy end up with the majority of digital currencies, for the same reason they end up with the majority of gold coins and central bank-issued currencies: they own the majority of the income-producing assets, so they have the income to buy assets such as crypto-currencies.

The Moral Foundation of Money

None of the existing money systems—gold and silver, printing paper money, central bank-issued credit money or existing crypto-currencies—address the root causes of inequality and poverty.

Though it is not explicitly stated, this is because money is considered to be apolitical and amoral, meaning it has no political or moral foundation.

But as I have shown, money is always and everywhere *intrinsically political* and thus it has a moral component that integral to its political nature.

Since none of the conventional systems of money creation and distribution address the origins of inequality and poverty, each is explicitly *immoral*.

The only way a system of creating and distributing money can claim to be moral is if it explicitly addresses the root causes of inequality and poverty, which is a lack of access to new money and income-producing capital.

The only way a system of money creation can directly address inequality and poverty is to bypass the state/central bank by distributing money directly to those at the bottom of the wealth/power pyramid. The only way such a decentralized system can distribute money with sustainable moral incentives is if *labor itself creates money*.

In other words, the only moral mechanism for creating money is to take the mechanism away from the central state and bank and make the creation of money *payment for productive labor*.

How can money be created by labor?

The answer is money can be created digitally upon confirmation that the productive work was indeed performed. Digital currencies have demonstrated that the technology already exists to create money in a decentralized way.

What is needed is a mechanism that ties the creation of money to the one thing people mired in poverty have, which is their time and labor.

This labor-based system of money creation and distribution runs completely counter to the conventional assumptions about money: that is must be issued by centralized authorities, that *sound money* (i.e. money that reliably holds its value) is apolitical and amoral, and so on.

That these ideological beliefs pass for certainties is certainly convenient for the elites that control money creation and distribution. In the carefully choreographed universe of the status quo, poverty has nothing to do with how money is created and distributed, even though poverty is the direct consequence of being outside the money creation and distribution machine.

The fact that every conventional money system generates poverty is attributed not to the money system but to external factors such as poor soil, an oppressive social system, lack of educational opportunities and so on rather than to the design of the money system itself.

I cannot imagine a more perfect protection for elites than the belief that money is disconnected from the mechanisms that concentrate wealth and power at the top of the pyramid. The ideal defense against charges that the dominance of the financial Aristocracy is immoral is to deny that the mechanisms of creating money have a moral foundation.

In essence, the argument that money is apolitical and amoral is equivalent to saying: we are wealthy and powerful not because the system is designed to concentrate wealth and power in our hands but because we are lucky, talented and/or divinely deserving.

Given the *intrinsic immorality* of centrally issued money, the only way to wrest control from elites is to take the power to create and distribute money away from them and give it to a decentralized system that distributes the money not to the few at the top but to the productive labor of the many.

This again raises the question: will the elites give up the very foundation of their wealth and power? Of course they won't; the only way they will relinquish the source of the wealth/power is when the status quo collapses.

This labor-based mechanism for creating and distributing money is a new form of *symbolic capital*. Since it is a new form of symbolic capital, is it unfamiliar, and prone to being rejected for that reason alone. My book *A Radically Beneficial World: Automation, technology and Creating Jobs for All* outlines in great detail how a new way of creating and distributing money to the 99.5% rather than to the .5% could work.

Chapter Three

The Eight Types of Capital

What is capital? Broadly speaking, capital generates value, which we measure as wealth.

Let's say a poor farmer gains the right to use a plot of land to grow crops which will be sold for a profit. The land is a form of capital, for without the land, no crops can be grown.

The farmer also needs seeds and tools to tend and harvest the crops (shovels, scythes, etc.), and perhaps fertilizer and pipes to carry irrigation water.

But the land, seeds and equipment are not enough to successfully harvest a profitable crop. The farmer also needs the knowledge of how to farm, a network of colleagues to help with the harvest and a market where the harvest can be sold. We call this knowledge, experience and expertise *human capital*, the network *social capital*, and the marketplace *cultural capital*.

If any of these forms of capital are missing, there will be no harvest and no profit.

There are two basic types of capital: tangible (physical) and intangible. Both are necessary.

Tangible capital:
1. Financial capital: money in cash, credit, etc.
2. Natural capital: the resources of the natural world including living capital (fish, trees, etc.) and resources such as soil, minerals and fossil fuels.
3. Fixed capital: machinery, tools, communications networks, etc.

Intangible capital:
4. Human capital: the intellectual and experiential capital needed to make the other forms of capital productive.
5. Social capital: the connections and relationships that enable productive collaboration and cooperation.
6. Cultural capital: the political and social institutions that enable broad-based increases in productivity.

7. *Symbolic capital* describes the conceptual tools that enable new ways of being productive. The concept of credit is an example of symbolic capital. If the farmer has no cash and must borrow money to buy the seeds and tools, the availability of credit is a form of symbolic capital.

8. *Infrastructure capital* is the result when all the other forms of capital work hand in hand. One way to illustrate infrastructure capital is to imagine a self-made billionaire being dropped into the desert populated by nomadic peoples who have no interaction with the global market economy. Our billionaire's wealth, skills, knowledge and social capital have no value because the infrastructure that supports these forms of capital is lacking.

Capital is ultimately the means of creating value. In the desert, the essential forms of capital are the knowledge of where to find the few water wells, and containers to store water while traveling.

What is valuable is by definition scarce. Sand has little value in the desert because it is abundant. What has value is water because it's scarce.

The Scarcest Capital Is the Most Valuable Capital

Not all types of capital are equal in terms of their impact on the prosperity of individuals and nations. The key is scarcity: which inputs to production are scarcest? The scarcest inputs will accrue most of the profits. Inputs include all forms of capital (cash, raw materials, tools, etc.) and labor.

Central banks have created tens of trillions of dollars, yen, yuan, euros, etc. in the past decade. This financial capital is now abundant (at least to financiers and corporations).

As a result of automation, human labor is also abundant; there are more people who want to work than there are jobs.

As the costs of digital technologies (software, 3-D fabrication, robotics and automation) decline and the capabilities of these technologies advance, conventional capital and labor have been *commoditized*, that is, turned into globally interchangeable commodities with little scarcity value.

Financiers can borrow yen, dollars or some other currency; central bank money is interchangeable. A factory can be built in China, Ireland or elsewhere; the products, location and workers are all interchangeable.

Commoditization makes all inputs interchangeable. Global labor has been commoditized because it no longer matters which workers assemble the goods, global capital has been commoditized because it no longer matters where the capital comes from, and globally produced goods, services and resources have been commoditized because it no longer matters where they come from or who produces them.

Factories producing televisions can be located anywhere and staffed with workers from anywhere; the money to build the factory can come from anywhere and the output (TVs) is interchangeable with outputs from other factories.

The profit that can be earned from capital and labor is based on the value premium that can be charged for scarcity; high profits flow to what's scarce, not what's abundant/commoditized.

Authors Erik Brynjolfsson, Andrew McAfee, and Michael Spence explain how innovative, practical ideas have become the scarcest form of capital in the digital age in a 2014 *Foreign Affairs* article, *Labor, Capital, and Ideas in the Power Law Economy*.

What will be scarce in the emerging digital economy are ideas that enable new products and services and radically reduce the cost of producing goods and services. The authors see *innovative ideas as a third form of capital*, with traditional capital and labor being the first and second types of capital.

In the taxonomy of capital described above, this third form of capital includes the various subcategories of intangible capital: human, social, cultural and symbolic.

We can summarize the authors' analysis in three points:

1. Digital technologies are radically reducing the need for human labor and the value-creation potential of traditional capital (land, fixed assets, finance and labor) globally.

2. Premiums flow to whatever inputs are scarce. Traditional labor and capital are no longer scarce; innovative, practical ideas are scarce. Ideas that enable new products, services, processes, etc. will harvest the majority of value (and profits).

3. This distribution of value/profits follows a power law, i.e. the *Pareto Distribution* in which the *vital few* with the third type of capital (good ideas) reap most of the rewards.

As a result of globalization and overcapacity, most inputs are no longer scarce, and so the value created by conventional labor and capital is trending down in every sector.

This mirrors the analysis of socio-economist Immanuel Wallerstein covered in Chapter One: for structural reasons, the yield on capital is declining and the cost of human labor is rising. As digital technologies get cheaper and more powerful, prices, the value of human labor and capital decline. Only the intangible capital of new ideas and processes become more valuable.

In the developed nations, companies such as Apple and Google are held up as examples of the power of new ideas to accrue outsized profits from new products and services.

But global high-tech giants are not the only example of the leverage of new ideas and processes. In the developing world, appropriate technologies created by new ideas and processes offer a much smaller-scale source of value creation. In a village without electricity, for example, capital that enabled the small-scale generation of electricity from a renewable source (flowing water, wind or sun) would have the greatest impact on well-being and productivity.

Ideas and tools that enabled the villagers to construct most of the tangible capital themselves and maintain the generator themselves would have more power than a one-time gift of the generator. The generator itself, though valuable because the financial capital to buy it is scarce, is only one type of the many forms of capital needed to maintain the system and make best use of the electricity. These are types of intangible capital: new ideas, processes and skills.

Productive, practical ideas become part of humanity's *best practices*, and the only way to alleviate poverty structurally is to distribute these best practices at near-zero cost and incentivize their adoption. While it is not possible to distribute fixed capital or resources at near-zero cost, the tools of intangible capital—knowledge, information and best practices—can be distributed digitally for near-zero cost. These forms of capital provide powerful leverage to make best use of whatever capital and labor are available.

We Optimize What We Measure

What we choose to measure and how we measure it is a specific type of symbolic capital. The process of selecting which data is measured and recorded, carries implicit assumptions with far-reaching consequences.

What we choose to measure reveals the limits of this form of symbolic capital.

Why does this matter? *Humans naturally optimize what is being measured and identified as important.*

If students' grades are based on attendance, attendance will be high. If doctors are told cholesterol levels are critical and the threshold of increased risk is 200, they will strive to lower their patients' cholesterol level below 200.

If we accept that growth as measured by gross domestic product (GDP) is the measure of prosperity, politicians will pursue the goal of GDP expansion.

If rising consumption is the key component of GDP, we will be encouraged to go buy a new truck when the economy weakens, whether we need a new truck or not.

If profits are identified as the key driver of managers' bonuses, managers will endeavor to increase net profits by whatever means are available.

The problem with choosing what to measure is that the selection can generate counterproductive or even destructive incentives.

This is the result of humanity's highly refined skill in assessing risk and return. All creatures have been selected over the eons to recognize the potential for a windfall that doesn't require much work to reap.

When humans were hunter-gatherers—our natural state for hundreds of thousands of years, compared to roughly 5,000 years of agriculture—those on the lookout for a calorie-rich windfall that didn't require a lot of work ate better (and had more offspring that survived) than those who failed to reap windfalls. In the natural world, such windfalls might be a tree heavy with ripe fruit or a beehive loaded with honey.

Calories were scarce, and work burns a lot of calories, so the ideal scenario for the hunter-gatherer is a windfall that can be harvested with a minimal investment of calories/effort.

In the abstract economy of the present, qualifying for a positive reward without investing too much effort is a windfall. As a result, whatever is measured sets up a built-in incentive to game the system (i.e. exploit short-cuts) or cheat to qualify for the reward with the least effort possible.

So if students are graded on attendance, and attendance is measured by the students signing in at the start of class, students can get the reward of a high grade by signing in and then sneaking away.

If students are graded on submitting homework daily, some students will extract homework from other students that can be copied with less effort than actually doing the work. Those seeking a windfall might use bribes or threats or blandishments to get the free homework, as the investment required to pursue these strategies is still smaller than that needed to do the homework.

If the grades are measured by a multiple-choice exam, some students will attempt to steal the answers ahead of the exam.

Compare these relatively easy-to-game thresholds to difficult-to-game tests such as long-hand answers to randomly selected questions assigned to each individual at the start of the exam. If the answers must be composed within the test period, it is essentially impossible to learn which questions students will receive beforehand and therefore impossible to prepare an answer (or pay someone else to answer) beforehand. Since the essay is written in the students' own hands, and each student has a different question, having others answer the questions during the test period is also nearly impossible.

Once the time and effort needed to game the system exceeds the investment required to learn the material, the incentives shift to learning the material with the least effort possible.

Notice that the system's cost of measuring data and enforcing compliance is correlated to the effectiveness of the enforcement and the value of the data. The lower the system's costs, the lower the compliance rate and the value of the data. Any system which makes compliance cheaper in effort invested than shortcutting the system will have high costs. The more effort invested in obtaining meaningful data, the higher the value of the data.

In our example, the cheapest measures of student performance—attendance, multiple-choice tests, etc.—do the poorest job of measuring actual student learning. To actually measure student learning requires significant investment in the process, and a careful analysis of what metrics best reflect real student learning.

There is a growing dissatisfaction in the economics field with the current measures of economic activity: GDP, unemployment, and so on. This dissatisfaction reflects a growing awareness that these legacy metrics do a poor job of capturing what is actually important in fostering sustainable, broad-based prosperity, what many call well-being.

Healthcare metrics offer a useful analogy. If cholesterol levels are a critical measure of health, then the medical community devotes its resources to lowering cholesterol levels below whatever threshold has been identified as critical. But what if a better overall yardstick of health and risk is the body mass index (BMI), which measures height and weight?

While there are limits to BMI (for example, some super-fit bodybuilders might have an elevated BMI, even though they are not fat), for the vast majority of people BMI is a useful measure of risk for cardiovascular and metabolic syndrome-related diseases such as diabetes.

Unlike measuring cholesterol, BMI does not require drawing blood; anyone with access to a tape measure and a cheap scale can calculate their BMI. Unlike cholesterol and blood pressure, both of which can be lowered with medications, BMI is difficult to short-cut. The only way to lower your BMI is to lose weight, which in the vast majority of people means losing accumulated fat via a disciplined regime of diet and fitness.

The status quo is based on legacy metrics that are misleading or counter-productive. The status quo has been optimized to gather these measurements and assign great meaning to them.

Does it make sense to optimize expanding consumption when resources are finite and the incentives to squander resources on unproductive consumption are so high?

If profits are the only metric that matter, and labor costs are rising for structural reasons, then why would private enterprise hire more workers when robots and software are cheaper and more productive in terms of boosting profits?

If we measure academic achievement by the issuance of a college degree, but the process of earning that degree does not measure real student learning, then what are we measuring with college diplomas? What we're really measuring is the students' ability to navigate an academic bureaucracy for four or five years. Since we're not measuring useful learning, we have no way to hold colleges accountable for their demonstrable failure to teach useful skills.

The key point here is *systemic success or failure arises from our choices of what to measure and what thresholds we set as meaningful.* Whatever we select to measure and deem important, participants will optimize their choices and behaviors to reach the rewards that are incentivized.

If we choose counterproductive metrics, we built perverse incentives into the system, incentives that guide the goals, strategies and behaviors of participants.

Rather than measure consumption and metrics that incentivize debt, what if we measure the well-being of each participant and the opportunities offered by their community? What if we measured doing *more with less* rather than consuming more? What if our primary measure of economic well-being was the reduction of inputs (resources, labor, capital, etc.) that resulted in higher output (increased well-being)?

How can we select metrics that productively measure well-being, sustainability and opportunity not just for elites but for every participant? What thresholds can we set that will create incentives for adopting best practices and appropriate technologies?

These questions help us see that to create a sustainable system that alleviates inequality and poverty, we must first choose metrics that create productive incentives for best practices and disincentives for fraud, corruption, waste and inefficiencies.

Chapter Four

The Limitations of the Market and the State

The status quo has two solutions for every problem: the market and the state. Whatever the market can't fix, the state can fix. These are the only recognized systems and the only recognized solutions.

While there is a role for the market and the state, these systems have built-in limits. The majority of life lies well beyond those limits. In very narrow spheres of human activity, markets and the state provide limited solutions. But beyond those narrow spheres, the market and the state become the problem, not the solution.

Attempting to solve every problem with the market and the state destroys the planet and the economy.

Limitations of the State and Universal Basic Income

Let's start by recalling that the state is ultimately dependent on the private-sector market economy for its revenues. State ownership does not mean state enterprises have detached from the market; the market prices every good and service, including those produced by state-owned enterprises.

If the state builds a factory to fabricate widgets, and there is low demand for widgets, the state's income from selling widgets won't cover the expenses of wages, operating expenses and capital costs (i.e. replacing worn out machine tools, etc.). The state can only cover the losses in two ways: it can subsidize the losing widget factory by taxing other enterprises or it can borrow money.

Neither is a sustainable solution. Eventually the state's losing enterprises absorb all the profit from the productive companies. This starves those companies of investment which causes them to become less productive and thus less profitable. Eventually the state's unprofitable companies bankrupt the entire state.

If the state fills the gap between expenses and revenues by borrowing money, the cost of servicing that debt eventually chokes off other more productive spending. Starved of productive spending, the state must either default on its debt or close the failing factories and fire their employees.

When people lose their livelihoods, the status quo solution is for the state to give them social welfare: cash payments, food stamps, free medical care, transportation subsidies, subsidized housing, etc.

The status quo solution to automation replacing human labor is Universal Basic Income (UBI), a guaranteed basic income paid to everyone regardless of their employment. Those with high-paying jobs would return their UBI to the state via taxes, while those with little to no paid work would be consumers, not producers. In this fantasy, robots do most of the work and humans are free to become artists, musicians, etc.

This is a fantasy for several reasons. Proponents of UBI never explain where the state will get the enormous sums needed to fund UBI, especially as profits and paid labor—the source of all tax revenues—decline.

The assumption that the owners of robots will reap more profits is false, for reasons explained above: software and robots are commodities that reduce costs and profits.

The assumption that people without livelihoods will naturally become artists and musicians is also false, for the reasons noted above: people need goals, purpose, meaning and positive social roles. Being a consumer provides none of these essentials, which are only generated by being a producer of value.

Proponents of UBI never examine the dysfunctional, socio-pathological realities of people on welfare, i.e. people currently receiving UBI via subsidies and other programs.

If we look at the incentives built into welfare programs such as UBI, we find that the incentives are all perverse: recipients have no skin in the game, so there are no incentives to build capital or take risks; instead, the free benefits curry dependence on the state. The social welfare programs fund just enough welfare to keep the recipients dependent on the state and politically passive—the modern-day equivalent of Roman bread and circuses.

Free money is incapable of incentivizing productive labor or the amassing of capital. This leads to a devastating conclusion: since state programs such as Universal Basic Income do not generate capital or positive incentives, *they institutionalize and perpetuate poverty rather than solve it.*

Limitations of the Market

Market economies reward profit, and this incentive is widely seen as the key to alleviating inequality. But profit only incentivizes a narrow range of behaviors, many of which are not productive or sustainable. For example, the profit motive incentivizes reef-fishing with dynamite (especially if you can strip someone else's reefs) and hunting the Bluefin tuna to near-extinction, as each fish is potentially worth tens of thousands of dollars.

The profit motive incentivizes misrepresenting goods and services (this investment is risk-free, etc.), designing in obsolescence so buyers are forced to replace the item, exploitive monopolies, price-fixing cartels, and externalizing environmental damage by polluting the air, rivers and seas which offloads the costs of production onto the general public while the profits remain private.

The market has no intrinsic mechanism to discover the cost of long-term consequences, such as the future value lost when forests are clear-cut or the long-term risks of routinely using pesticides on crops. *This is a flaw it is inherent to the market's core mechanism of discovering price with current supply and demand.*

The market has no mechanism to calculate the long-term *opportunity cost* to pursuing short-term profits: what other potentially higher-return long-term investments were abandoned in the pursuit of short-term profits. This distortion of opportunity costs is a second intrinsic flaw.

When a credit-based global market economy is introduced into traditional local economies, the incentives change from sustainability to extracting the highest possible profit from the environment before someone else does so. When the market economy expands credit (which it generally does, as credit is even more profitable than trade), participants are incentivized to borrow money to buy luxuries that they could otherwise not afford.

Cheap credit profoundly skews our appraisal of opportunity costs, as the total future costs of servicing the debt are masked by the modest monthly payments.

This intrinsic inability to discover the real cost and value of anything, not just in the present but in the future, cannot be eliminated by regulation. As noted above, what we measure has to be changed at the foundation of symbolic capital.

Markets have a third flaw: they are easily exploited by elites seeking income that arises from control rather than from producing goods and services. Incomes arising from control—of land, borders, the marketplace itself—are known as *rentier incomes*, as they are a form of rent (or more properly, a tax) paid to elites who create no value.

The fourth and most important flaw is that a *market that measures profit as the sole goal offers few incentives for adopting best practices or building capital*. The seas are being stripped of fish to maximize short-term profits, while the capital lost when the ocean ecosystem has been destroyed goes unnoticed and unmeasured in the status quo.

Since the status quo doesn't measure life-cycle costs, the future value of what's been destroyed to reap short-term profits, well-being or sustainability, the result is a destructive tyranny of maximizing profit today.

The fifth flaw is that markets are inherently prone to boom and bust cycles, as the exploitation of whatever is profitable unleashes a tsunami of income, debt and external costs (pollution, overfishing, etc.) which crashes as the resource is depleted or undermined by competition from afar.

Participants are left with debt and external costs they have no way to pay, as their income has dried up along with the profitable trade.

The sixth flaw is that markets have no way to incentivize tasks that do not create a direct and immediate profit—for example, monitoring the community's reefs to stop exploitation by others.

It is presumed the state will naturally step in to perform these unprofitable tasks, but the state—dominated by self-serving elites and state functionaries—has no incentive to pay for profitless tasks serving those without political power, especially if the tasks limit the profits of powerful interest groups.

There is nothing in the structure of markets that incentivizes sustainable prosperity for all. The belief that the *invisible hand* of self-interest will inevitably foster a sustainable economy is magical thinking. Self-interest is indeed a powerful motivation, but it responds to whatever incentives are present. If perverse incentives are present, pursuit of self-interest leads to self-destruction.

A transparent marketplace for goods, services, labor, risk and credit is not a stand-alone solution to poverty—it is only one part of a larger integrated solution of sustainable secure income for all, the distribution of intangible capital and productive incentives.

The real engine of universal opportunity and prosperity is intangible capital that generates a productive set of metrics, incentives and tools that benefit all rather than the few at the top of the wealth/power pyramid.

The Market, State and Labor

It is widely assumed that the market will always create plenty of jobs as a function of supply and demand. But if we examine the declining return on capital and the rising costs of labor from the perspective of an employer, we reach an entirely different understanding of the market for labor.

The owner of a free-market enterprise has no built-in need to hire employees unless more employees are necessary to increase profits. Recall that labor costs are increasing everywhere due to the four structural forces listed in Chapter One, and as a result it is at the top of the list of costs the owner seeks to trim. If automation can be purchased for less than the cost of employees, that substitution raises profits even if sales and margins are declining.

The owner has every incentive to cut labor costs, either by reducing the number of employees, hours employees are paid, hourly pay scale or by transferring labor's overhead costs (healthcare, pensions, etc.) to the state.

The ideal arrangement for owners of private enterprises is zero labor costs and plenty of customers with money to spend. That this is a contradiction has long been widely recognized: if private enterprise doesn't hire enough employees, who will have the money to buy their goods and services? This was one of Henry Ford's stated objectives in raising the pay at his auto factories in the early 20th century.

It is an article of faith in conventional economics that the opportunities to reap profits are intrinsically unlimited, and therefore we can always count on entrepreneurs creating new and profitable enterprises that will hire people to increase profits. What is not understood is the potential to replace human labor with digital and robotic technologies is as unlimited as opportunities for profit.

While highly profitable labor-intensive businesses occasionally sprout, two factors mentioned in Chapter One are limiting the expansion of paid work: one is that profits are increasingly difficult to reap for structural reasons, and the second is that reducing labor costs by replacing workers with technology is incentivized by rising labor costs and declining costs of technology.

Businesses that increase profits by increasing human labor are outliers in a system which incentivizes replacing human labor as one of the few ways to maintain profits.

Those who imagine that the state can hire every person without a private-sector job are overlooking the fact mentioned above: the state's revenues ultimately flow from the private-sector economy. State ownership does not mean the enterprise has escaped the need to make a profit. Borrowing money to pay workers to dig holes and then fill them is not a sustainable solution, as rising debt and stagnating tax revenues eventually eat the state alive.

Neither the market nor the state has any solution for the systemic replacement of human labor by automation and commoditization's relentless downward pressure on profits.

The Limits of Profit as a Determinant of Value

In a market economy, all investment must turn a profit. It makes no sense to invest time and money in projects that lose money. Everyone who pursues losing projects eventually runs out capital and goes bankrupt.

The problem with making profit the sole determinant of value is a great many projects cannot possibly turn a profit, yet they offer tremendous yield and value.

One example is a safe community bikeway. Studies have found that safe bikeways—bike lanes that are separated by barriers from autos— encourage multi-generational bike traffic that in turn increases local shop revenues. Bicycling removes vehicles from the road, reduces smog, and generates health benefits for bicyclists that reduce social healthcare costs. Each of these yields is significant; together, they offer outstanding positive returns for the relatively modest cost of building safe bikeways.

There is no way to make a profit on building bikeways, unless bicyclists are charged money for every use. Such a fee structure would present a huge disincentive for bicyclists, and undermine the entire purpose of the bikeway.

The conventional response to the multiple benefits of safe bikeways is to suggest the state pay for the bikeways to promote the common good. This idealized view of the central state overlooks the political nature of all state decisions: the state, firmly in the grasp of self-serving elites and vested interests, serves those interests, not the common good.

Since the status quo holds rising consumption as the highest economic good, bikeways that reduce purchases of fuel, vehicles and medical services are resolutely negative. Due to the shortsightedness of what we measure, there appears to be no significant benefit to investing capital in safe bikeways: reducing future healthcare costs isn't counted, and neither is reducing smog and traffic congestion. Bikeways reduce what we measure—GDP—and so they are anathema to the status quo.

The single most important characteristic of state spending is its dependency on private-sector profits and the employment those profits enable. Even state borrowing is ultimately dependent on private-sector taxes, as the tax revenues pay the interest on state debt.

An enormous share of human activity is not profitable, nor does it benefit the elites and vested interests that control state spending. The market economy can only perform work that is profitable; what is intrinsically profitless is left undone.

The state, beset by competing demands on its limited revenues from various elites and vested interests, will spend just enough *bread and circuses* to keep the populace politically passive. The rest of state revenues are devoted to paying interest on the state's ballooning debt and rewarding the elites and vested interests that control the state.

Those who naively believe the potential for profit can solve all economic and social problems are engaged in magical thinking. So are those who believe the state can pay for everything that is not profitable, for the state is ultimately limited by private profits and private employment, both of which are declining for structural reasons.

The Unsustainability of State Social Welfare Spending

The status quo is based on the faith that profits and employment will always expand, and as a direct result so will state revenues. As we have seen, these dynamics have reversed, and both profits and employment are in structural decline.

The conventional belief is that the central bank and state serve as buffers for the ups and downs of private-sector markets. When leverage, credit and speculation reach an extreme, the business cycle requires a cleansing of bad debt and a reduction in speculation. As credit contracts, investment and credit-based spending also shrink and the economy enters a recession.

Keynesian doctrine holds that the central bank should lower interest rates and flood the financial sector with credit (liquidity), and the state should borrow and spend more to compensate for the sudden decline in private demand. In the Keynesian view, the state can pay people to dig holes and fill them or build bridges to nowhere; it doesn't matter what the state spends the borrowed money on.

This buffering of the business cycle is a temporary support which is withdrawn as the economy magically recovers from the contraction of credit and writedowns of bad debt.

But for all the structural reasons described here, the economy is not healing itself as Keynesians expected. Rather, the extreme monetary and fiscal policies of the Keynesians—in effect, *doing more of what has failed spectacularly*—have deepened the structural problems rather than cured them.

As profits and wages contract, so too do state revenues. In response, the state increases its borrowing. As employment and wages decline, the state's social welfare spending increases dramatically as state revenues decline.

Since the conditions underpinning the economy have changed, the expected recovery cannot occur. But trapped in the intellectual box canyon of Keynesian dogma, the state and central bank have no choice but to sink deeper into debt as the only available means of funding rising social welfare spending.

Eventually the interest on the debt chokes state spending and private investment, which sets in motion a self-reinforcing feedback loop of higher taxes, declining investment and productivity and rising interest payments on ballooning debt.

Although the central banks can create money out of thin air, these tricks of financialization can only delay the inevitable default on state debt or the devaluation of the state's currency.

Adding fuel to this consuming fire is the insatiable demand of the populace for more state social spending, listed by Wallerstein as a structural driver of higher taxes and higher labor costs.

The cycle of the state increasing social welfare spending at an ever-faster rate and funding the increase with debt is a no-exit strategy: it can only lead to default and devaluation of the state's currency. Once faith in the currency is lost, the state may continue issuing $1,000 payments to recipients, but the recipients will find the $1,000 no longer buys a loaf of bread.

The tragic irony is the state social spending that was intended to ease poverty will inevitably end up greatly increasing poverty as debt collapses the state's ability to fund social welfare with more debt.

The Neoliberal/State Fantasy of Taxable Profits and Wages

The status quo (neoliberal) fantasy is that every good and service can become a profitable market of transactions and wages which generate tax revenues for the state.

Consider two households as an example.

Household #1 eats most of its meals in cafes and restaurants, and whatever meals are eaten at home are packaged—frozen pizza, mixes, etc. This household sends its children to private schools and pays for after-school care and enrichment lessons. A maid is paid to clean the house, and a gardener is paid to care for the yard. The maintenance of the family vehicles is done by others, and a dog walker is paid to walk the family pet. All home maintenance is done by professionals. Mom and Dad pay personal trainers for their fitness regimes, and pay monthly fees for gym memberships.

Household #1 is the private sector's fantasy: every activity generates revenue and profit. This is the state's fantasy, too: every activity generates transactions, profits and wages that are all taxed.

Household #2 is in a traditional village. The children go to the local school, and the parents scrape up what little cash is available to pay school fees and buy supplies. All meals are prepared at home with food that is homegrown or obtained by barter. All household tasks are done by the household members, including home maintenance. Any labor that cannot be performed within the household (for example, repairing the household's old motorbike) is bartered by in-kind labor or homegrown food.

Virtually all of the activity in Household #2 is done without paying anyone.

Household #2 is the neoliberal nightmare: there is essentially no potential for profit in this village because nobody has enough income to pay for anything beyond low-profit basics such a few school supplies. Needs are met without generating profit, wages or taxes paid to the state.

This village is also the state's worst nightmare, because with no transactions, profit or paid labor, there is no activity that can be taxed.

Measured by conventional metrics of gross domestic product (GDP), the village produces near-zero GDP. By these same metrics, Household #1 generates an enormous amount of GDP.

Which is more sustainable, given that profits and paid labor are both in structural decline?

Is conventional GDP measuring what is actually important in each household?

The problem with the neoliberal/state fantasy is that only the top 5% of American households can afford the lifestyle of Household #1 without going deeply into debt.

The idea that the market and state can transform every aspect of human activity into a profitable venture that generates tax revenues for the state is not just detached from reality—it ignores what's actually important: sustainable well-being.

The Destabilizing Consequences of Globalization

It is not possible to coherently discuss the market, labor and the state without discussing financialization—the substitution of credit expansion and speculation for productive investments in the real economy—and its sibling: globalization.

Globalization is the result of the neoliberal push to lower regulatory barriers to trade and the expansion of credit in overseas markets. The basic idea is that global trade lowers costs and offers more opportunities for capital to earn profits. This expansion of credit in developing markets creates more employment opportunities for people previously bypassed by the global economy.

Though *free trade* is often touted as intrinsically positive for both buyers and sellers, in reality trade is rarely free, in the sense of equally powerful participants choosing to trade for mutual benefit. Rather, "free trade" is the public relations banner for the globalization of credit and markets that benefit the powerful and wealthy, not the impoverished.

As we shall see, financialization and mobile capital exacerbate global imbalances of power and wealth.

Trade is generally thought of as goods being shipped from one nation to another to take advantage of what 18th century economist David Ricardo termed *comparative advantage*: nations would benefit by exporting whatever they produced efficiently and importing what they did not produce efficiently.

While Ricardo's concept of free trade is intuitively appealing because it is *win-win* for importer and exporter, it doesn't describe the consequences of financialization and the *mobility of capital*. In a world dominated by mobile capital, *mobile capital is the comparative advantage.*

The mobility of capital radically alters the simplistic 18th century view of free trade.

What do we mean by mobile capital? Capital—cash, credit and the intangible capital of expertise—moves freely around the globe seeking the highest possible return. As noted previously, the prime directive of capital is to expand; capital that fails to expand will shrink. If the contraction continues unchecked, the capital eventually vanishes.

Globalization is the ultimate expression of capital's prime directive: expand profits by seeking the highest available return on capital invested anywhere on the planet.

In today's world, trade cannot be coherently measured as goods moving between nations, as capital from the importing nation often owns the productive assets in the exporting nation. If Apple owns a factory (or joint venture) in China and collects virtually all the profits from the iGadgets produced there, this reality cannot be captured by the simple trade model described by Ricardo.

Trying to account for trade in the 18th century manner of goods shipped between nations is nonsensical when components come from a number of nations and profits flow not to the nation of origin but to the *owners of capital.*

Based on the antiquated model of trade between nations, the Apple iGadget creates a $200 trade deficit between the U.S. and China when it lands on an American dock. But this doesn't account for the fact that components for the device were manufactured in five different nations, or that the majority of the value of the device is in the intellectual capital: the software, the interface and the design.

Once these factors are considered, it's been calculated that as little as $10 of the value of every
Apple product actually ends up in the Chinese economy. Virtually all the profit flows to Apple in Cupertino, California, not to joint venture partners in China or the workers who assembled the components in China.

Expanding profits is by moving production to locales with lower labor costs is known as *labor arbitrage.* Arbitrage is the process of exploiting the difference in prices of labor, currencies, goods, services, assets, interest rates or credit.

In today's globalized version of "free trade," mobile capital can arbitrage the varying costs of labor, currencies, interest rates, taxes, environmental regulations and political favors by shifting capital between nations.

In the global economy, trade is not conducted between equals; those with access to the unlimited credit of financialization can outbid domestic capital for assets, labor and political favors.

The mobility and scale of capital give it outsized influence in small, credit-starved local markets.

Mobile capital can borrow billions of dollars (or equivalent) in one nation at low rates of interest and then use that money to outbid local entrepreneurs in other nations with few sources of credit. Mobile capital, with its essentially unlimited line of credit, can overwhelm the local political system, buying favors and cutting deals to limit costs and competition. Local political elites are no match for this influx of money which is so much larger than the local economy. Local elites are soon co-opted, and people starved for cash income are easily recruited as labor.

Local assets—priced for the local economy where credit and cash are both limited—are snapped up on the cheap by global capital, and sold for immense profits.

Credit—scarce in traditional self-sufficient economies—offers maximum leverage to global capital, which can borrow money in distant markets at low costs and use the cash to outbid local buyers to snap up local resources that are still cheap compared to the resources in other globalized markets.

The influx of credit also fuels a destabilizing explosion of credit-based consumption in the local economy, causing people with little experience with credit to become over-indebted.

As the over-indebted default, their land and other possessions are confiscated by offshore lenders, further impoverishing the local populace and enriching global capital.

Mobile capital can exploit resources and cheap labor until the resource is depleted or competition cuts profit margins. At that point, mobile capital closes the factories, fires the employees and moves on.

Where is the "free trade" in a world in which the *comparative advantage* is held by mobile capital? And what gives mobile capital its essentially unlimited leverage? Central banks, which issue nearly-free money to banks which funnel the cash to corporations and financiers, who can then roam the world snapping up assets and arbitraging global imbalances with low-interest money.

There's nothing remotely "free" about trade based on capital flows generated by central bank liquidity.

States also play the currency arbitrage game, pursuing policies that cause their currency to lose value, which makes their exports cheaper in overseas markets.

Those holding currencies that are increasing in value can in effect buy assets on the cheap in nations whose currency is declining in value. This gives mobile capital double advantage, as it can borrow money in one currency and convert it to another currency that is gaining purchasing power.

This mobility of capital is an enormous benefit to the owners of the capital, but it creates extraordinary instability for those who are not as mobile. When mobile capital encounters anything that reduces profits—higher taxes and rising labor costs, competition or restrictive regulations—it closes factories and fires workers in that locale and shifts to another locale with greater opportunities for high returns.

The workers left behind have limited means to replace the lost wages, and the local state often has few resources to repair any damage left by the exploitation of resources. The advantage of mobility is reserved for capital, and to the relatively limited cohort of workers who can immigrate to other nations to find work.

This illustrates two key *ontological characteristics* of financialized globalization: *perpetual instability and a never-ending cycle of boom and bust* as capital sparks rapid development in one locale and then moves elsewhere once profits decline.

The scale of global capital is difficult to grasp; trillions of central bank-issued dollars, euros, yen and renminbi are sloshing around the global economy, seeking low-risk profits.

Capital has no loyalty to anything but its own expansion, and the damage it leaves in its wake is of no concern to the owners of capital.

There are even less visible consequences to the globalization of markets, capital and labor. Once goods and services are priced globally, local supply and demand no longer set the local price. As my colleague Mark Gallmeier has observed, consumer prices can rise even if there are deflationary surpluses in the local economy because price is set by global supply and demand. As a result, measuring inflation and deflation locally is meaningless in a globalized economy.

This globalization of price—for goods, services, credit and currencies—continually creates imbalances that fuel a perpetual instability that gradually impoverishes every sector other than global capital, which being mobile, can exploit the imbalances for its own profit.

Who benefits over the longer term from the permanent instability and boom-and-bust cycles of this arrangement?

Ownership Capital and Shared Capital

We need to make a critical distinction between two basic types of mobile capital: *ownership capital*, in which owners of mobile financial capital buy resources and assets to maximize their own gain, and *shared capital*, which is intangible and can be freely shared with others on a global scale.

In general, *ownership capital* seeks ownership of material assets such as mines, forests, land and factories, and control of intangible capital such as intellectual property, markets and regulations. Where ownership is not possible, capital seeks joint ventures, leases or other means of control that are the equivalents of ownership.

In contrast, *shared capital* is entirely intangible. An open-source mobile-payment application is an example; the software is offered freely to everyone with a mobile device. The ownership of the rights to the software is less important than its availability and low cost (the lowest cost being free).

Broadly speaking, shared capital is digital knowledge, tools or processes—globally accessible *best practices*. These include open-source software, freely available instructional videos and networks that enable shared problem-solving.

The globalization of shared capital is a great boon, as it makes best practices available to everyone with access to a networked device. Shared capital, being digital, is mobile, low cost and it cannot be withdrawn at the whim of its originator: ownership is distributed among all who use it.

This is a radically different model from the mobile financial capital described in the previous section. Where mobile ownership capital is ontologically exploitive, shared capital is ontologically enriching, as it enables everyone with digital access to use the vast range of intangible capital (i.e. best practices) for their own benefit.

The Tyranny of Price

The neoliberal notion of free trade assumes that *price is the only metric worth measuring*: people want a lower price, regardless of the consequences of what was done to deliver the lower price. I call this reduction of complex processes and consequences to the single metric of price *the tyranny of price*, for it generates a destructive obsession with price at the expense of the consequences of the way the product was produced.

If the lowest-price product will only last a third as long as a slightly higher-priced product, is the lowest-priced product really the cheapest over its entire life-cycle? The answer is of course no; the product with the higher initial price-tag is actually the lower-cost product because it lasts much longer.

If I buy the cheapest food because it is the cheapest option, what are the consequences of that choice to my health later in life? If the low-quality, low-cost food leads to chronic illnesses that are horrendously costly to treat, the initial low cost was illusory if we look at future costs and consequences.

If we can buy food from overseas cheaper than we can grow food ourselves, the tyranny of price leads us to stop raising food locally since it makes no sense to do so based on price.

That this loss of productive skills and land leaves us entirely dependent on mobile capital's arbitraging of imbalances in global food production is not included in the price of the food. The catastrophic consequences of that fragile supply chain from overseas being disrupted are also not in the price.

As noted before, markets base price solely on current demand and supply. All the dominoes of future costs and consequences are invisible in the tyranny of price.

Clearly, what we measure in price is fatally flawed, and this failure leads to poorly informed, destructive choices. In effect, *price is inadequate information and knowledge*.

The Fundamental Failure of the Market and State

We identified four global models that the status quo holds up as solutions but which have become our most destructive systemic problems.

1. An economic model of expanding consumption in a world of finite resources

2. An economic model that relies on wages to distribute the output of an economy

3. A political-economic model of centralized states managing economies

4. An economic model that depends on ever-expanding credit

Each of these models is breaking down for structural reasons.

We next considered the moral and financial consequences of the way money is issued by central banks/states to the top of the wealth/power pyramid.

We then examined the eight types of capital and the consequences of our choices of what we measure.

We completed our analysis by examining the limitations of the market and the state, and the destructive consequences of mobile capital and globalization.

We are now in a position to see that the source of inequality and poverty is the centralization of wealth and power in finance and the state--specifically, the institutionalization of centralized control of money and credit and the leverage this centralization of power and wealth offers self-serving elites.

The difference between a despot who skims $70 billion from his impoverished populace and financiers who skim $70 billion from their proximity to the money spigots of the central bank is simply one of details: the basic mechanism—centralized control of money, credit and the state leveraged by a self-serving elite—is the same.

To understand why this is so, we turn to the *ontological imperative* of a system or institution.

The *ontological imperative* of the state is to expand its control. The State has only one mode of being, expansion. It has no concept of, or mechanisms for, contraction.

From the state's point of view, everything outside its control poses a risk. The only way to lower risk is to control everything that can be controlled.

State control institutionalizes *moral hazard*, the separation of risk from gain. The key characteristic of moral hazard can be stated very simply: People who are exposed to risk and consequence act very differently than those who are not exposed to risk and consequence.

Those working in the state's agencies do not suffer any real consequences should the agencies fail to achieve their public purposes. State employees don't lose their jobs, benefits or pensions if the agency fails; they have no real skin in the game.

Those receiving state social welfare also have no skin in the game. The state's dysfunction is fed from both ends: by those managing the state and those dependent on its welfare/ Universal Basic Income.

The moral hazard generated by the centralized state has two negative consequences. Authors Franz Kafka and George Orwell addressed these consequences in their writings.

A lawyer by training and practice, Kafka understood that the more powerful and entrenched the state bureaucracy, the greater the collateral damage rained on the innocent, and the more extreme the perversion of justice.

Orwell understood the State's *ontological imperative* is expansion, to the point where it controls every level of the marketplace and society. Once the State has expanded beyond the control of the citizenry, it becomes the target of those seeking to leverage its power to their own personal advantage.

The *ontological imperative* of capital is to secure profits by limiting competition and gaining access to the central bank's money spigot. The cheapest way to secure profits is to influence the state to limit competition and be first in line to the central bank's money spigot.

The *ontological imperative* of privileged elites is to skim as much of the national income as possible.

This is how nations fail: centralized power attracts elites who then steer the state and its central bank to serve their interests, at the expense of everyone below the apex of power.

We can now understand Wallerstein's characterization of the current system: as "a particular historical configuration *of markets and state structures* where private economic gain by almost any means is the paramount goal and measure of success."

This centralized marriage of state and market is the source of inequality and poverty. Simply put, there is no profit in alleviating inequality and poverty, so there is no incentive in either the market or the state to address inequality and poverty. There are also no consequences to those inside the state if its bureaucracies fail to alleviate inequality and poverty. The lowest-cost, lowest-risk method of dealing with poverty is to distribute enough bread and circuses (welfare and Universal Basic Income) to keep the poor politically passive and distracted by cheap entertainment. This is what is incentivized, and so this is the output of the status quo.

Those who believe that the vested interests benefiting from the status quo will surrender their power and perquisites are indulging in magical thinking. As a result, alleviating inequality and poverty will have to come from outside the status quo.

As we have seen, the mechanism of distributing national income with wages is broken and cannot be fixed; technology's replacement of human labor is an essentially limitless process that is still in its infancy.

The mechanism of increasing prosperity by increasing consumption of finite resources is broken.

The mechanism of depending on ever-expanding debt to fund current consumption is broken.

The mechanism of central banks/states creating and distributing money is broken.

The mechanism of concentrating political power is broken.

Not only are these mechanisms broken; the system's components—central banks, central states, global markets—are *the wrong unit size*, meaning that they are incapable of producing anything other than the outputs they currently generate: the consolidation of wealth and power by self-serving elites, and broken mechanisms that lead to systemic failure.

The digital technologies we call the Internet also have an *ontological imperative*: creatively destroy monopolies and every effort to limit information, dissent and the feedback of consequence. To the degree the centralized state is a monopoly that limits information, dissent and consequence to protect itself, it too will be dismantled by the Internet.

Chapter Five

The Failure of Economic Orthodoxy

In this section, we cover the failings of the two dominant economic theories and the poverty of authenticity, self, purpose and meaning that defines the status quo.

To understand why we need a new system and a new source of meaning, we must first understand these five dynamics:

1. The pathologies of markets
2. The pathologies of neoliberal financialization
3. The pathologies of the state and centralized wealth and power
4. The pathologies of consumerist capitalism (permanent adolescence)
5. The pathologies of derealization (loss of authenticity)

Neither of the two dominant economic ideologies, capitalism or Marxism, can account for these intertwined pathologies, or grasp that they are the inevitable result of the status quo.

The Failure of the Either/Or Orthodoxies of Capitalism or Marxism

The conventional understanding how economies function is based on a simple theoretical binary: there are only two analytic camps to choose from, capitalism or Marxism. What is striking is that both systems have failed in the real world, for reasons that are largely invisible to each system's apostles and believers.

Orthodox (what we might call classical) capitalism focuses on the potential of self-interest, free markets (the primary components of Adam Smith's famous *invisible hand*) and international trade to create wealth for participants and nations. Please note the word *potential*: these attributes do not broaden wealth as an automatic force of nature;

they can all exist in a system that impoverishes the many to benefit the few.

Orthodox Marxism focuses on the self-destructive nature of capitalism's drive to maximize financial-political power and eliminate labor costs and competition. These lead to the death spiral of fewer workers, diminishing profits and the disruption of the social order.

In the alternative system Marx envisioned, workers owned the means of production (factories, mines, shipping, railroads, etc.). As a result of this ownership of the productive assets, everyone would share more or less equally in the wealth being generated.

Neither of the two orthodoxies foresaw the dominance of centralized political and financial power, or the marriage of these concentrations. Though both systems recognize that political and financial power arises from the issuance of money and credit, neither one recognizes the immorality of centralized money/credit creation.

Both systems rely on theories that see labor as the source of value—the labor theory of value (LTV). Neither system can account for modes of production where labor is a diminishing input as automation replaces not just human muscles but human intelligence. Neither system has any theoretical way to address the end of work described in Part One, and neither addresses the fundamental input left out of the classic LTV formula: $c + L = W$ (capital plus labor equals value).

The missing input is what author John Michael Greer terms the Wealth of Nature—everything extracted from the *natural economies* of the Earth that function without human intervention. This vast wealth awaiting our extraction and exploitation is not valued by either system beyond the market price of the extracted commodities.

Neither orthodox capitalism nor orthodox Marxism recognizes the value of the 90% of the fish that are killed and tossed into the sea by trawlers because they have no value in the human marketplace. In both systems, getting rid of the "worthless" fish is a cost. Neither system proposes any way to measure the value of ecosystems that are destroyed, the opportunity cost of destroying natural systems or the long-term value of ecosystems we are disrupting.

Both orthodoxies accept the market's reduction of complex ecologies to price. Both reject *ecology* as the guiding model of *how the world works* in favor of the *machine model* of quantified inputs and outputs that can be adjusted to achieve the desired expansion of consumption and capital.

The *totality of value*—future consequences, opportunity costs, the wealth of natural systems, and the value of everything that cannot be distilled down to price by current supply and demand—is not even recognized, much less acknowledged.

Both systems assume prosperity requires an eternal expansion of consumption—that infinite growth of consumption on a finite planet is not just possible but necessary. The concept of Degrowth—that our goal should be to consume less and make better use of what we extract from the natural economy—does not exist in either orthodoxy.

In effect, both economic orthodoxies are blind to the two key realities governing our future: automation and the limits on consumption imposed by a finite planet.

The Pathologies of the Market

I have endeavored to describe the unique benefits of markets and also their inherent limitations: they are very good at what they do, but there is much they cannot do as a consequence of their reductionist nature.

The five intertwined pathologies discussed earlier can be understood as having three basic sources. The first is the reductionist nature of markets. The second is the particular structure of the state-capitalism that is the dominant mode of production across the globe. The third set of pathologies arises from the status quo's attempts to mask the failure of the system with falsified data and fake narratives.

Marx understood that capitalism's ontological imperative is to continually dismantle and disrupt economic, political and social orders as a byproduct of maximizing profit and expanding capital. Marx described the consequences of this dynamic in his famous phrase, "all that is solid melts into air."

In orthodox capitalism, this constant destruction of the fabric of social and even familial life is a byproduct of *creative destruction*, economist Joseph Schumpeter's phrase. Any attempt to limit this creative destruction limits capitalism's ability to adopt greater efficiencies and expand innovation and capital.

Capitalism inevitably disrupt existing *modes of production*—the systems that coordinate capital, labor and the distribution of the goods and services being produced—as more profitable modes of production are developed.

In other words, markets don't set out to destroy existing modes of production and social orders as their goal: the market's goal is to maximize profit and expand capital. The disruption of existing modes of production and social orders is a byproduct of replacing existing modes of production with those that are more efficient and more profitable.

Markets have no incentives or mechanisms for creating social orders to replace those that have been dismantled, other than the market itself.

The *teleology of the market* (teleology = the system's intrinsic goal or end point) is that every order that is dismantled becomes a market or is organized to serve the market: politics, the social fabric, even family relations.

This substitution of markets for the interwoven social orders that were destabilized spawns a wealth of mutually-reinforcing pathologies.

In the previous section, we briefly discussed the market's ruthless reduction of the *totality of value* and the Wealth of Nature down to price.

Markets reduce human ecologies—political, economic, social and familial orders—in the same manner. Both natural and human orders are destabilized and destroyed as the market's reductionist *machine model* replaces the *ecology model.*

This mechanistic reduction strips away complex layers of interactions and feedbacks, and replaces this ecosystem with a simplistic *moral imperative*: whatever yields more profit and expands capital *by any means* is superior and thus inevitable.

Just as the deep-sea trawler operating to maximize profits dumps 90% of its catch as the "worthless" (and cumbersome) byproduct of catching the 10% with high market value, so too does the global trawler of capitalism dump existing social orders as cumbersome obstacles to higher profits and expanding capital.

Since the market has no way to value the fish with no market value, it is rational to dump them overboard. Since the market has no way to value the ecosystem that has been disrupted, it is rational to destroy the ecosystem to harvest the valuable fish.

This dismantling of existing orders is not even understood as destruction; the market reduces the process of destruction to a *cost of doing business*.

Not only do markets not recognize any value in the social orders being destroyed; they are viewed as hindrances to more profitable modes of production.

Just as unmarketable fish don't register as having any value in the natural world, democracy and political legitimacy do not register as having value in the market; indeed, democracy and political legitimacy are reduced to forces that could potentially disrupt the most profitable modes of production.

Given the imperative of the market, democracy and political legitimacy are hindrances rather than treasures, and this is the source of the status quo's *teleological imperative* to maintain facades of democracy and political legitimacy in the public sphere.

Acutely aware that the narratives underpinning the social order operate as a powerful secular mythology, the status quo devotes tremendous resources to the manipulation of public perception.

This conscious shaping of our experience has been described by author and psychiatrist R.D. Laing as the *politics of experience*. The goal is to create a compelling shadow-world that projects the mythology of democracy and broad-based prosperity.

The cost of generating this shadow-world of fake data, fake prosperity, fake promises, fake freedoms, fake democracy and most especially fake authenticity are a necessary expense, much like dumping the dead fish overboard: it would be nice to dispense with this cumbersome shadow-world, but it is part of harvesting the maximum profit possible.

As workers are stripped of livelihood, that doesn't register as either an input or an output in the market. If those dispossessed ex-workers coalesce into a force that disrupts the status quo, suppression and/or bribery become an annoying but inescapable cost, much like dumping worthless fish overboard.

68

Marx described the alienation of the worker from the product of his labor, and the resulting loss of meaning. This psychological insight into work as the fundamental source of purpose and meaning falls on deaf ears in both economic orthodoxies. Since alienation and meaning cannot be quantified, these essential qualities of the human experience are discounted or simply ignored by the profession of economics.

The key point here is that the pathologies generated by the market are not just present in economic structures—they are internalized within each individual as a loss of purpose, meaning, self-worth and selfhood.

Once the mythology constructed with fake data and fake narratives is internalized by each participant, the failure to create value in the market is perceived as a personal failure rather than the failure of the system.

This is akin to the fish that is about to be dumped overboard as waste thinking that it was his fault that his life was being squandered as a byproduct of higher profits.

This internalization feeds a vast self-help industry, as those who has been dumped overboard blame their own inadequacies for their loss of livelihood. While it is self-evident that each participant must accept responsibility for their choices and actions, the sense of being worthless reflects the system's pathologies.

I call this internal impoverishment *social defeat*, as the person who has been cast overboard as having no value is not just economically defeated, he/she is *socially defeated*. Stripped of the financial rewards of work, the unemployed are also deprived of purpose, meaning and a positive role in society.

This internalization of failure is convenient for the status quo, as it numbs individuals' awareness of the system's pathologies. The human desire for meaning now serves a market for self-help, where the marginalized bid for inspirational books and therapies.

Just as gravity is the rarely noticed force that governs our material world, *permanent insecurity* is the background force in the world of work, as self-worth and a livelihood are contingent on maintaining value in the market. Once the market for one's labor vanishes, financial and psychological insecurity are the inevitable result.

Once again we must stress that the pathologies of permanent insecurity are not the market's goal; they are the byproduct of the market throwing everything but maximizing profit overboard as worthless.

This ceaseless disruption of the social order generates an deep-seated insecurity that the status quo can never erase. Those whose labor no longer has value in the market are tossed on the rubbish heap of society and supplied with enough bread and circuses (now called Universal Basic Income) to suppress public expressions of discontent.

Capitalism excels at destabilizing economic, political and social orders and distributing *social defeat* to everyone who is marginalized, but it cannot create a replacement social order other than a market in which price is discovered solely by current supply and demand.

That this artificial, unsustainable and deeply impoverished system is incapable of constructing a healthy, productive social order is of no concern to those profiting from the ascendency of the market.

Derealization and the Destruction of Authenticity

The word *derealization* is essential to understanding how the pathological nature of the status quo has been obscured by a carefully contrived fog of mythology.

Derealization is a clinical term that describes a psychological state linked to cognitive and psychiatric disorders. The person experiencing derealization may feel related symptoms such as depersonalization and intense anxiety.

In my analysis, derealization is not a clinical term describing an individual's psychiatric dysfunction; it describes the process of replacing authenticity with a facsimile that serves the status quo. The purpose of derealization is to cloak the pathologies of the status quo so the few can continue to benefit at the expense of the many. This substitution depends on our willingness to accept superficial data points and public-relations references to social mythologies as authentic.

Thus the claim that only data has meaning in economics is the equivalent of the claim that maximizing private gain is the sole measure of value. The reduction of all economic life to data points derealizes what actually matters in economics: sustainable well-being.

Derealization—replacing the true with the fake—is the air we breathe. Thus we have fake data, fake markets, fake competition, fake oversight, fake rule of law, fake democracy and one false choice after another masquerading as legitimate choice.

The essential task of derealization is to cloak the *dominance of concentrated wealth and power*.

Simply put, the first priority of concentrated wealth and power is to tear the heart out of classical capitalism: competition in a transparent market in which all participants have the same access and information.

This is not just the logic of maximizing private gain—it is an absolute necessity, for only by eliminating competition and transparent markets can those at the top of the pyramid expand profits.

Neoliberalism is a powerful tool of derealization, as everything that cannot be reduced to a market is marginalized, colonized or indentured to serve a market.

The language of neoliberalism takes pieces of classical capitalism and transforms them into a moral system that is presented as the solution to every social or economic problem. Thus the solution to any problem is to make a market in which maximizing private gain is the highest good.

The language of market speculation— maximizing return on investment, etc.—presents markets as a universal problem-solving machine.

That these concepts do not necessarily apply to every circumstance in human experience is alien to neoliberalism. Even more alien is the idea that these concepts act as a sort of linguistic poison that reduces everything in human existence to a speculative drive for private gain.

Once a system has been infected by neoliberal terminology, it is effectively derealized: no sense can be made of anything except as the workings of a speculative market that places a premium on maximizing private gain.

Once again I must stress that markets serve a valuable role in human economic life. But neoliberalism doesn't simply make room for markets; they *are the system*, and the teleological end-point of this

71

system is concentrated wealth and power that rigs the market to benefit the few at the expense of the many.

The *teleology of financialization* is to maximize the speculative profits reaped by turning every asset into collateral that rationalizes a vast expansion of debt and leverage. The end-state of financialization is financial servitude to debt, a state I call *neofeudalism*, as the fundamental relation is debtors who are in lifelong servitude to those who own the debt.

This is feudalism but without the stability and relative security of feudalism. In neofeudalism, the debt-serfs cannot depend on lifelong employment or shelter. The modern debt-serf has no real security until he reaches old age, and that security is contingent on the state being able to borrow unlimited money to fund the retirement and healthcare of a rapidly aging populace.

There is nothing in the system to limit debt to youth or middle age; financialization inevitably generates lifelong indebtedness. Thus Social Security may be less about financial security for the elderly and more about providing elderly debtors with enough income to service their debts.

In other words, the neofeudal version of serfdom is more contingent and less secure than its Old-World model. Neofeudal serfs toil not for nobility that is visible in the manor house, but for an invisible Financial Nobility that owns all the debt and the political power to protect its wealth.

The implicit moral imperative of neoliberalism is very simple: maximizing profit is the highest good. Once we accept this moral imperative, it naturally follows that turning everything into a market in which participants seek to maximize their private gain is the ideal solution to all problems.

The primary outputs of the neoliberal status quo are derealization, predation, neofeudalism, inequality, social defeat and what my colleague Simon Hodges terms *productive wastage*—the production of needless or useless products and services.

Much of humanity's success as a species stems from our extraordinary ability to habituate to extremes and make them ordinary. This adaptive ability is not without cost, however: we adapt to the extremes of dysfunction, oppression, exploitation, etc., but we lose our emotional bandwidth to do more than merely survive.

The chronic anxiety resulting from the gulf between *what we're told we're experiencing and what we're actually experiencing* is the cost of habituating to environments that are dysfunctional and pathological.

This derealization manifests in everyday life many ways: eating disorders, difficulty sleeping, passivity, lack of engagement with real life, inability to maintain meaningful relationships, reliance on drugs, inability to concentrate, low-intensity rage, chronic frustration, depression, anxiety disorders and so on.

One way to understand the depth of this systemic derealization of the human experience is to ponder the vast distance between conventional economics and all the pathologies that the status quo generates. Economics presents itself as a bloodless science akin to physics, but the reality is economics is neither bloodless nor a science. Rather, it is the primary engine of derealization, mystifying interactions and relationships so that few can even grasp the consequences of the status quo's economic construct of neoliberalism, markets and the state.

These pathologies manifest in every institution within the status quo and within each participant in the institutions and the markets they serve.

The Institutionalization and Internalization of Perverse Incentives

The perverse incentives of the status quo are not formally institutionalized; rather, they infect the each institution and every participant, guiding their motivations and behaviors without any formal direction at all.

In the status quo, the goal of every individual working in an institution is to maximize their gain—wages, benefits, vacation time, pension payouts, etc.—without regard to the purpose of the institution. If the institution fails in its purpose, this is of no consequence to insiders seeking to maximize their private gains within the institution.

To the degree that fulfilling its purpose siphons funds from wages, pensions, vacation time, etc., fulfilling the purpose may actively detract from each insider's private gains. In this case, the rational choice is to subvert the institution's effectiveness lest the maximization of private gain be limited.

In effect, fulfilling the founding purpose of the institution is at best secondary, and at worst an active impediment to maximizing private gain.

The leadership of the institution has a dual motivation: maximize their private gain and insure the power and budget of the institution expand, as these are *institutional forms of capital*. Should these forms of capital shrink, the private gains of those within the institution are imperiled.

This teleology ignores the purpose of the institution; once again it is secondary at best, and at worst it is reduced to a public-relations façade to mask the pillaging of the institution's budget by the individuals within.

These perverse incentives are internalized by the individuals within the institution from their first moment of contact.

Is it any wonder that institutional failure is the norm in the status quo?

Those being served by the institution are equally incentivized to game the system to maximize personal gain. Cheating on exams, paying others to write class essays, fudging numbers to qualify for benefits, falsely claiming disability—these are all not just incentivized by the status quo, they are effectively institutionalized by the status quo.

Institutionalized Powerlessness and the Crisis of the Individual

Most people working within dysfunctional institutions do their best to keep the institution operating, and they naturally resent their institution being labeled dysfunctional, as it calls into question the value of their work. Their role in the institution is the wellspring of their identity and self-worth, and attacks on the institution are easily personalized into attacks on their self-worth.

74

This is understandable, as the need to affirm the value of one's work is core to being human.

Several factors work against the affirmation of an individual's value in centralized institutions. While some institutions are better run than others, hierarchical institutions are ontologically in conflict with the human need for affirmation of one's value, purpose and meaning.

While each individual seeks to be recognized as a valuable member of a productive community, the institution is designed to enforce obedience to the hierarchy and compliance with the many rules governing the institutional machinery.

To soften the enforcement of obedience, institutions offer various blandishments of recognition: employee of the month, etc. Hierarchical organizations that must compete for workers, such as technology firms, will actively court their employees with Friday parties and various bonding events to generate a sense of purpose and community.

But stripped of public-relations cheerleading, these ploys are deeply inauthentic. They aren't designed to create a real community, but to simply soften the enforcement of obedience with superficial recognition of the human need for recognition and belonging. Their real purpose is to mask the employees' powerlessness.

Why do individuals accept powerlessness? The institution offers them what is scarce: financial security and a position that offers an identity and sense of belonging.

But there is an intrinsic conflict between the institution's need for obedience and the individual's need for authentic community, purpose and identity.

Within small work groups, camaraderie between the employees nurtures authentic community. But this is not the result of the institution; rather, the bonding occurs despite the institution.

This conflict is deepened by the dysfunction that arises from the structure of all centralized hierarchies. In effect, institutions bribe individuals with the security of a wage and a position, but the individual can never be fulfilled by a bribe or a position that is intrinsically powerless.

Even those in positions of leadership are powerless to change the dysfunctions that arise from its structure. The ontology of hierarchical institutions is to restrict the power of any individual, as individual initiative poses a threat to the institution's core dynamic, which is the *commodification of all human labor* within it. People must be interchangeable within the institution for the hierarchy and rules to function. Every teacher can be replaced with another teacher, every administrator can be replaced with another administrator, and so on.

This ontological conflict between the individual and the institution is complex. The institution offers various facsimiles of recognition, but the individual remains powerless and interchangeable. The institution claims to be improving, but it remains dysfunctional and incapable of reforming itself.

The impossibility of meeting individuals' needs for autonomy and affirmation manifest in a number of ways; here are five examples.

The first is the individual's powerlessness to change anything of consequence within the institution. Everyone knows it is dysfunctional, but even those in positions of nominal power are unable to effect any real change.

The second is the difficulty of feeling positive about one's role in an institution that has clearly lost its way and squanders talent and capital as its default setting.

The third is the internal costs of complying with perverse incentives that strip away integrity, idealism and faith in the value of the institution's output.

The fourth is the way in which rising costs and burdensome rules of compliance narrow the room to maneuver within the institution. There is little room for innovation or meaningful reform because the budget is devoted to maintaining the status quo, and compliance soaks up time, talent and capital.

The fifth is keeping up with the ever-shifting sands of political compliance, as metrics of productivity change with each administration. What was adequate before may no longer be good enough.

The institution is designed to enforce compliance of its employees as a means to fulfill its core purpose. But there are few effective mechanisms for transformation within centralized institutions; each additional rule of compliance is added to a pile that is rarely reduced. As the costs of compliance and legacy structures increase, innovation is crowded out.

Even worse, innovation inevitably threatens someone's share of the budget and power pie, so any innovation immediately arouses powerful enemies within the institution.

As a result, the institution becomes increasingly sclerotic and self-protective, and the narrowing room to maneuver frustrates the most idealistic and talented, who either quit or are forced out as threats.

Those who choose to remain resign themselves to cynical conformity or they simply stop caring. Neither is conducive to valuing one's work.

In other words, institutions self-select for those most adept at maintaining the illusions of productivity, empowerment, etc., while maintaining the structure that guarantees dysfunction and artifice.

I call this conflict between centralized, hierarchical institutions and human needs *the crisis of the individual* because the institution is unaffected by its failure to meet the human need for affirmation, autonomy and community; the only crisis that afflicts the institution is the loss of its funding.

The crisis of the individual is not limited to institutions. Indeed, it can even more acute outside institutions. Affirming one's value and identity are difficult in an institutional setting, but they become nearly impossible for those who have no paid position in the workforce.

Like institutional dysfunction, the crisis of the individual is as unrecognized as the air we breathe. It is assumed to be not just the way the world works, *but the only way it could possibly work.*

But these pathologies are not gravity; they result from a specific arrangement of markets, central states/banks and the neoliberal imperative that maximizing private gain is the highest good.

Where does the status quo channel this human need for selfhood, autonomy and authenticity? The system offers one source of selfhood, identity and self-worth: what we consume, buy, wear and present to the world.

With limited opportunities to develop an authentic self within the institutions that control much of everyday life, consumerism is held out as the one source of self that is accessible and that we can control.

The Consumerist Destruction of the Authentic Self

77

Just as there is a cost to maximizing private gain, there is a cost (measured in authenticity) to the elevation of consumption as the primary expression of identity, autonomy and self-worth. As noted in Part One, the *teleology of consumerism* leads to what I call *permanent adolescence*—the state of mind of an insecure teen with a credit card and a desire to establish a high-status identity by becoming a consumer rather than a producer.

An authentic self that is pursuing self-development has no place in status quo economics, since authenticity, selfhood and self-development cannot be quantified as part of Gross Domestic Product (GDP). The concept of an authentic self has no place in neoliberalism, which only registers the maximization of private gain, or in financialization, which only recognizes leverage and speculation in service of maximizing private gain.

Consumerism offers an attractive simulation of authenticity: we are encouraged to express our true self by displaying brand-name signifiers of our status, aspirations and identity. Those without the means to purchase a consumerist expression of selfhood suffer social defeat; they have no status or selfhood.

The substitution of consumer signifiers for authentic selfhood is only the first layer of damage. Consumerism nurtures an emotional isolation and immaturity that leaves many people without the tools needed to handle criticism, collaboration and the normal pressures of the workplace.

The ontological imperative of consumerism is *the only self that is real is the self that is purchased, signified and projected*. The teleological end-state of consumerism is narcissism and self-absorption.

Christopher Lasch, author of *The Culture of Narcissism: American Life in an Age of Diminishing Expectations* identified the ontological essence of narcissism: a fear of the emptiness that lies at the very core of consumerism.

Consumerist marketing glorifies the *projected self* as the *true self*, encouraging self-absorption even as it erodes the resilience which enables internally generated integrity and authenticity—the essential characteristics of adulthood.

Personal gratification goes hand in hand with self-absorption, a fragile sense of self and an identity that is dependent on consumerist signifiers and the approval of others: in other words, *permanent adolescence.*

Authentic selfhood is impossible in a state of permanent adolescence, which is based on a constantly decaying feedback of external approval.

Consumerism only recognizes a few human emotions: fear (of being seen as *less than you are* rather than *more than you are*), anxiety (that you are not displaying the trendy signifiers of the moment), desire, acquisitiveness, gratification and a trivialized tribal identity derived from displaying Brand X. The values and emotions derived from productive work, cooperation, self-development and positive social interactions simply don't register in consumerism.

Once again we find that the pathologies resulting from consumerism are taken for granted, as if living through consumption is the natural order and *the way the world must work.*

The authentic self does not register in consumerism; it literally goes unrecognized. A self that does not reflect Its aspirations and appetites in consumption is a shadow, just as social relations that are not market-driven do not register.

Just as maximizing private gain is the sole imperative, consumerist signifiers are the sole source of selfhood, autonomy and self-worth. This is the inevitable consequence of markets and neoliberalism: those who have no institutional position, no market value and no consumerist signifiers are invisible. In terms of maximizing private gain and consumerism, they cease to exist.

The Structure of Collapse

The end-state of unsustainable systems is collapse. Though collapse may appear to be sudden and chaotic, we can discern key structures that guide the processes of collapse.

Though the subject is complex enough to justify an entire shelf of books, these six dynamics are sufficient to illuminate the inevitable collapse of the status quo.

1. Doing more of what has failed spectacularly. The leaders of the status quo inevitably keep doing more of what worked in the past, even when it no longer works. Indeed, the failure only increases the leadership's push to new extremes of what has failed spectacularly. At some point, this single-minded pursuit of failed policies speeds the system's collapse.

2. Emergency measures become permanent policies. The status quo's leaders expect the system to right itself once emergency measures stabilize a crisis. But broken systems cannot right themselves, and so the leadership is forced to make temporary emergency measures (such as lowering interest rates to zero) permanent policy. This increases the fragility of the system, as any attempt to end the emergency measures triggers a system-threatening crisis.

3. Diminishing returns on status quo solutions. Back when the economic tree was loaded with low-hanging fruit, solutions such as lowering interest rates had a large multiplier effect. But as the tree is stripped of fruit, the returns on these solutions diminish to zero.

4. Declining social mobility. As the economic pie shrinks, the privileged maintain or increase their share, and the slice left to the disenfranchised shrinks. As the privileged take care of their own class, there are fewer slots open for talented outsiders. The status quo is slowly starved of talent and the ranks of those opposed to the status quo swell with those denied access to the top rungs of the social mobility ladder.

5. The social order loses cohesion and shared purpose as the social-economic classes pull apart. The top of the wealth/power pyramid no longer serves in the armed forces, and withdraws from contact with the lower classes. Lacking a unifying social purpose, each class pursues its self-interests to the detriment of the nation and society as a whole.

6. Strapped for cash as tax revenues decline, the state borrows more money and devalues its currency as a means of maintaining the illusion that it can fulfill all its promises. As the purchasing power of the currency declines, people lose faith in

the state's currency. Once faith is lost, the value of the currency declines rapidly and the state's insolvency is revealed.

Each of these dynamics is easily visible in the global status quo.

As an example of *doing more of what has failed spectacularly*, consider how financialization inevitably inflates speculative bubbles, which eventually crash with devastating consequences. But since the status quo is dependent on financialization for its income, the only possible response is to increase debt and speculation—the causes of the bubble and its collapse—to inflate another bubble. In other words, *do more of what failed spectacularly*.

This process of doing more of what failed spectacularly appears sustainable for a time, but this superficial success masks the underlying dynamic of *diminishing returns*: each reflation of the failed system requires greater commitments of capital and debt. Financialization is pushed to new unprecedented extremes, as nothing less will generate the desired bubble.

Rising costs narrow the maneuvering room left to system managers. The central bank's suppression of interest rates is an example. As the economy falters, central banks lower interest rates and increase the credit available to the financial system.

This stimulus works well in the first downturn, but less well in the second and not at all in the third, for the simple reason that interest rates have been dropped to zero and credit has been increased to near-infinite.

The last desperate push to *do more of what failed spectacularly* is for central banks to lower interest rates to below-zero: it costs depositors money to leave their cash in the bank. This last-ditch policy is now firmly entrenched in Europe, and many expect it to spread around the world as central banks have exhausted less extreme policies.

The status quo's primary imperative is self-preservation, and this imperative drives the falsification of data to sell the public on the idea that prosperity is still rising and the elites are doing an excellent job of managing the economy.

Since real reform would threaten those at the top of the wealth/power pyramid, fake reforms and fake economic data become the order of the day.

Leaders face a no-win dilemma: any change of course will crash the system, but maintaining the current course will also crash the system.

Institutions also prioritize their own preservation, and as a result resources are siphoned from fulfilling the purpose of the institution to maintaining its budget. The core operations of the institution decay and aggressive public relations are substituted for actual accomplishments.

The initial stage of collapse is decay: services become unreliable; shortages appear, households react defensively by hoarding essentials and cash, and the state increases its repression of dissent.

The only way to quiet disgruntled insiders, elites and state dependents is to print more money to reflate speculative bubbles and fund more state spending. If this expansion of the money supply does not increase the production of goods and services, the inevitable result is the devaluation of the currency, i.e. a loss of purchasing power we experience as inflation: our money buys less every day.

As the state increasingly relies on borrowing to fulfill its promises, a self-reinforcing feedback loop takes hold: the more money the state borrows or prints to pay its obligations, the greater the currency's loss of purchasing power. This forces the state to print/borrow ever greater sums, which further erodes the value of the currency.

If we look at history, we note that this process of devaluation rarely if ever reverses.

The loss of social cohesion and common purpose and the decline of social mobility are less visible than devaluation but equally difficult to reverse.

Again referring to the lessons of history, enduring empires maintained high levels of social mobility: those of humble birth had multiple pathways to wealth, power and influence.

When social mobility is lost, the status quo not only loses the talent of those denied access to the top rungs, it also enlarges the pool of ambitious outsiders whose energy and ambition are turned against the status quo.

When the privileged class locks up all the top rungs for its cronies, the status quo crumbles under the weight of incompetence, infighting, inefficiency and wasted resources, while the best and the brightest drop out of the economy or seek outlets for their ambition elsewhere.

The process of collapse is uneven and unpredictable. The status quo can decay for quite some time before systems break down, and occasional bursts of sound leadership can buy time. External shocks such as energy shortages or war can trigger the collapse of increasingly fragile but seemingly stable regimes.

The key takeaway here is the process of collapse is inevitable once these six dynamics take hold. Superficial reforms can buy time, but the status quo is caught on the horns of a dilemma: deep, structural reform will collapse the system, and maintaining the present course will also lead to collapse.

Why the Status Quo Is Beyond Reform

We have now reached the point where we can understand why the status quo is beyond reform: if the foundations of the system are eliminated, the system collapses. For example, if central bank interventions ceased and interest rates were allowed to float higher, the stock and bond markets would crash once the central bank supports were withdrawn. This crash would destroy much of the wealth of the privileged class and decimate the pension funds of the middle class.

If debt no longer expands, the system crashes as debt-fueled consumption declines. If the state no longer borrows immense sums every year to fund its obligations, state dependents arise in revolt.

The foundational systems of the status quo are interdependent. If one crashes, the entire system topples.

1. An economic model of expanding consumption in a world of finite resources

2. An economic model that relies on wages to distribute the output of an economy

3. A political-economic model of centralized banks/state managed economies

4. An economic model that depends on ever-expanding credit to fund consumption and the state

Reform fails for a self-evident reason: since these four systems are the problem, not the solution, reform would have to replace these unsustainable systems with more sustainable alternatives. But the disruption of any of these systems—ever-expanding wages to support ever-expanding consumption fueled by ever-expanding debt supplied by an ever-expanding central bank/state—fatally disrupts the entire status quo.

Yet for all the reasons outlined above, maintaining the status quo as is (i.e. no structural reforms) also guarantees collapse.

Reforms that change the foundations of the system will bring it down, yet the only way to save the system from collapse is to change its foundations. There is no escape from this no-exit dilemma.

Well-meaning reformers believe that adding more layers of regulations to centralized systems will fix what's broken. This is magical thinking, for superficial reforms that add cost without changing the foundations can only speed the decay and collapse of the system.

To review:

The belief that automation will create more jobs than it destroys is a fantasy.

The belief that profits will rise as automation is commoditized is a fantasy.

The belief that infinite expansion of consumption is possible on a finite planet is a fantasy.

The belief that debt can indefinitely expand at a rate that exceeds the expansion of wages and the production of goods and services is a fantasy.

The belief that an economy can borrow its way to prosperity is a fantasy.

The belief that devaluing a nation's currency will lead to prosperity is a fantasy.

The belief that the central state can expand indefinitely as the economy it depends on for revenues declines is a fantasy.

The belief that central banks can create money out of thin air and use that money to fund state debt indefinitely as the economy stagnates is a fantasy.

The belief that distributing new money and credit to the top of the wealth/power pyramid will solve inequality and poverty is a fantasy.

In conclusion: the belief that the status quo is sustainable is a fantasy.

The Way Forward

The consensus view is that the collapse of the status quo would be a global catastrophe. I hope after reading this book you now realize the collapse of the status quo is necessary to save what's left of the planet and clear the way for more sustainable systems to arise.

The decay phase of the status quo (i.e. the present) offers us a magnificent opportunity to fashion alternative systems that operate in the shadow of the status quo, making use of systems such as the Internet and mobile telephony. Alternative systems can arise without challenging the status quo; indeed, sustainable, decentralized systems offer open-minded elements of the status quo new models and new partners.

I lay out a fully integrated global alternative called the Community Labor Integrated Money System (CLIME) in my book *A Radically Beneficial World: Automation, Technology and Creating Jobs for All*. I invite you to explore CLIME as a sustainable, decentralized, global alternative to the doomed status quo.

Solutions abound. We just need to reach for them.

Charles Hugh Smith
Berkeley California
April, 2016